Celestial Echoes

Joe Anthony

NewDelhi • London

BLUEROSE PUBLISHERS
India | U.K.

Copyright © Joe Anthony 2025

All rights reserved by author. No part of this publication may be reproduced, stored in a retrieval system or transmitted in any form or by any means, electronic, mechanical, photocopying, recording or otherwise, without the prior permission of the author. Although every precaution has been taken to verify the accuracy of the information contained herein, the publisher assumes no responsibility for any errors or omissions. No liability is assumed for damages that may result from the use of information contained within.

BlueRose Publishers takes no responsibility for any damages, losses, or liabilities that may arise from the use or misuse of the information, products, or services provided in this publication.

For permissions requests or inquiries regarding this publication, please contact:

BLUEROSE PUBLISHERS
www.BlueRoseONE.com
info@bluerosepublishers.com
+91 8882 898 898
+4407342408967

ISBN: 978-93-7018-121-2

Cover design: Yash Singhal
Typesetting: Namrata Saini

First Edition: April 2025

Preface

It is a book of interesting themes from the Sacred Scripture expressed in poetry. The poems are on a variety of topics presented in different sections. These deal with the Lord's teachings, important events that have occurred and influenced humanity, prominent Biblical personalities who have contributed in various ways to further God's plan for man's existence, the Passion and death of Jesus, virtues and qualities God expects human beings to cultivate, the purpose and meaning of life, and a variety of such topics.

Many people make it a point to read some verses from the Holy Bible every day Reading them in poetic form could add interest and enjoyment. Children can easily memorize them as these poems are simple in expression, rhythmical and melodious to the ear. These can create greater interest in reading the Sacred Scripture and the enjoyment and benefit derived could be more sublime and more productive.

Joe Anthony

About the Author

BOOKS
BY
JOE
ANTHONY

Joe Anthony had been a teacher of English in reputed schools in Kolkata, Chandigarh and New Delhi in India and in Senior Secondary Schools in the Ministry of Education in Muscat, the Sultanate of Oman. After 40 years of teaching he retired and now lives with his family in Gurgaon, Haryana, India. He employs his time in creative writing, especially poetry, for his personal satisfaction and for the inspiration of others.

Other books of poems to his credit are A QUEST FOR THE SACRED, THE SACRED REVEALED, and SOULFUL SYMPHONIES.
Email: joeanthony45@gmail.com

www.joeanthony.co.in

THIS WORK IS DEDICATED

To the Greater Glory of God the Almighty

And to Proclaim His Profound Messages

Table of Contents

1. Impressive Events 1
   1. Jesus is Tested 2
   2. Escape to Egypt 4
   3. After An Endless Wait 6
   4. I Baptized Him 8
   5. Feeding Five Thousand 10
   6. A Memorable Wedding 12
   7. Jonah Flees From God 14
   8. The Transfiguration 16
   9. The Temple of God 18
  10. Valley of Bones 20
  11. What His Star Reveals 22
  12. He Calms the Sea 24
  13. Jesus Rides a Colt 26
  14. Laborers in the Vineyard 28
  15. Ten Lepers Were Healed 29
  16. The Parable of the Two Sons 30
  17. The Wicked Tenants 32
  18. The New Bethlehem 33
  19. A Reed in the Wind 35
  20. The Storm Was Furious 37

2. "What is Truth?" Pilate asked Jesus. 39
  21. God's Immensity 40

22.	On the Fabric of Creation	42
23.	The Ultimate Sacrifice	44
24.	The Cosmic Temple	46
25.	Painted In Poetry	47
26.	His Word Is Alive	48
27.	The Blood of the Lamb	50
28.	Do Not Enter Sodom	52
29.	Jesus' Second Coming	54
30.	Let The Children Come	55
31.	He Fills Every Space	57
32.	The Chalice and The Womb	59
33.	Broken And Scarred	61
34.	A Voice in the Wilderness	63
35.	Salt of the Earth	65
36.	His Masterpiece	67
37.	The Human Soul	68
38.	Step Into the Sacred Space	70
39.	Sacraments Have Power	71
40.	If I Could Touch	73
41.	Yahweh's Chosen	75
42.	Born in a Stable	77
43.	He Breathed Love into Life	79
44.	His Omnipresence	80
45.	His Warning Thundered	81
46.	Be Generous	82

3. Dogmatic Teachings of Jesus 83

47.	You are My Favorites	84

#	Title	Page
48.	Come to Me	86
49.	The Widow's Mite	88
50.	Blind Leads the Blind	90
51.	The Power of His Blood	91
52.	The Withered Arm	93
53.	Take My Yoke Upon You	95
54.	A Theocentric Treasure	96
55.	Follow Me	97
56.	Celebrate The Passover	99
57.	Be Holy as I am Holy	101
58.	A Profound Mystery	102
59.	Revealed to Children	104
60.	Hold on to His Cross	106
61.	A Tree and Its Fruits	108
62.	Woe to You	110
63.	Ten Virgins	111
64.	The Most Precious Love	112
65.	We Let Down the Net	113
66.	Call to Holiness	114
67.	Lay Your Hands	116
68.	He Heard Me Call	118
69.	Harsh Reminders	120
70.	Who is the Greatest	121
71.	If Jesus is Lost	122
72.	The Need to Expiate	123
73.	Who's My Mother	124
74.	Atrocious Indictment	125
75.	Net Full of Fish	127

76.	New Wine in Old Wineskins	129
77.	A Wedding Invitation	130
78.	Is Divorce Lawful	131
79.	Hold on to My Hand	132
80.	They Questioned Jesus	134
81.	I'm Not Here for Peace	136
82.	Searching for Jesus	137
83.	The Eye of a Needle	138
84.	He Came to the Rescue	140
85.	Your Nourishing Food	141
86.	The Vital Principle	143
87.	The Weed in the Crop	144
88.	Pray Without Ceasing	145

4. Biblical Personalities ... 147

89.	Hail My Lady	148
90.	The Carpenter's Son	150
91.	John the Baptist	152
92.	Two Expectant Mothers	154
93.	The Good Shepherd	156
94.	My Guardian Angel	158
95.	Simeon the Prophet	160
96.	Daughter of Phanuel	162
97.	Joseph the Just	164
98.	Mary of Bethany	166
99.	The Disciples of Emmaus	168
100.	The Prodigal Son	171
101.	Sons of Thunder	174

102. The Holy Spirit	176
103. The Pharisee and The Publican	178
104. The Man at the Pool	179
105. The Shepherds	181
106. Elizabeth	183
107. Simon of Cyrene	184
108. The Magi	186
109. Cain and Abel	188
110. Bartimaeus the Blind Man	189
111. Paul the Apostle	191
112. The Stone in the Sling	193
113. The Woman at the Well	195
114. The First Martyr	197
115. The Rich Fool	199
116. The Widow and The Judge	200
117. Veronica	202
118. Zacchaeus	204
119. Samuel's Calling	206
120. St. Jude	208
121. The Widow of Nain	210
122. Women in the Gospels	211
123. The Betrayer	213
124. Abraham's Sacrifice	215
125. The Holy Rosary	217
5. The Lord's Passion	**219**
126. Garden of Gethsemane	220
127. Judging God	222

128. Scourging	224
129. Crown of Thorns	226
130. Behold the Nails	228
131. The Ultimate Insult	230
132. Nailed to a Cross	232
133. At His Death	234
134. Knock of the Lance	236

6. Mesmerizing Experiences 237

135. To The Wilderness	238
136. The Relentless Hound	241
137. Your Ways are Unusual	243
138. Endless Bliss	244
139. An Unusual Trip	245
140. A Fruitful Search	246
141. To the Wooded Mountains	248
142. The Stain of Silence	250
143. A Perfect Pilgrimage	251
144. We Could Only Mourn	253
145. Strange are Your Ways	255
146. A Soul in Turmoil	257
147. Asking for Mercy	259
148. Keep Going	260
149. A Fire Within	262
150. Blessed are They Who Can Sing	263
151. Cling On	264
152. My Query to the Waves	266
153. No Reason to Hesitate	267

154. A Smile is Like a Flower	269
155. Discerning our Need	272
156. Life Slips Out	274
157. The Statue of Compassion	275
158. The Little Shrine	277
159. Be An Amplifier	279
160. Impossible to Describe Heaven	280
161. Destiny	282
162. Pushing Boundaries	284
163. God's Mode of Expression	285
164. The Touch of Sunshine	286
165. Suffering and Salvation	288
166. My Precious Bird	289
7. Embalmed with Scriptural Fragrance	**291**
167. Craving for Peace	292
168. Prefer to be Hidden	294
169. Sin is the Skin	296
170. Sealing Scars	297
171. His Concept of God	299
172. Some Love the Desert	300
173. A World of Simplicity	302
174. An Act of Compassion	304
175. Joy and Sorrow	305
176. Youngsters of Today	306
177. The Angelus	308
178. Offer Him a Shoulder	309
179. The Mystery of Death	311

180. The Wet Pebble	313
181. Under His Wings	315
182. The Process of Healing	316
183. True Justice	318
184. Which Way to Choose	320
185. The Bell Tolls	322
186. Glittering Tears	323
187. Time or Space	325
188. The Language of Conscience	327
189. At the Mouth of Hell	329
190. No Time to Die	330

8. Beauty of a Soul in Grace 331

191. Messages in Her Smile	332
192. She was a Jewel	334
193. The Scar of the Tear	335
194. A Melodious Symphony	337
195. Her Apprehension	338
196. A Resilient Life	340
197. Distraught and Lost	341
198. The Chalice of Pain	343
199. In Your Presence	344
200. Get Down to Your Knees	347
201. He Kills the Sting of Pain	349
202. When She Lost Her Mother	351
203. He Was a Mystic	353
204. Pleading For Aid	354
205. Attitude to Pain	356

206. Your Warm Smile 357

9. God and Man – A Unity 359

207. Render an Account 360
208. To Sit At His Feet 361
209. When I'm On My Way 363
210. Talk to Him Without Delay 365
211. In the Throes of Pain 367
212. He Made Me Eternal 369
213. You are Prodigal 370
214. The Altar of the Cross 371
215. The Holy Sacrifice 372
216. The True Bread 374
217. Waiting for the Call 375
218. Called to a Benigne Scene 376
219. Fill Me with Your Grace 378

1. IMPRESSIVE EVENTS

Certain events in the Holy Scripture are more prominent and persuasive than others because they influence us more. Here are a few of them that will stir the depth of every heart and urge it to react positively.

1. Jesus is Tested

'You're the son of God they say,
Prove it so, I pray,
Tell these stones to change to bread
With it you can be fed'.

'Man lives not on bread alone
Of which he has outgrown,
More important is the sacred Word
Uttered by the mouth of God'.

'You're now standing at the top of the temple
On its very pinnacle,
Throw yourself down, for it's assured
Your angels will stand guard'.

'You know very well what is written
You have read it often,
Do not put your God to the test.
It is beyond your limit'.

'Kingdoms of the world to you I render
In their glory and splendor,
These are yours if you bow down
You'll then own the crown'.

'Get away from me, you wicked one
For your name is Satan,
Worship me and serve me alone
Or from my sight be gone'.

Ashamed of failure and being scolded
Without delay he fled,
Angels came and gladly attended
And Jesus' ordeal ended.

2. Escape to Egypt

An angel knocked at the door of his dream,
Joseph awoke and listened to the scheme:
He was to head for Egypt that instant
With Mary and his newborn infant.

Sneaked out in secret, merged with the night,
Travelled with speed and vanished from sight;
Herod's on a mission to kill their child
To his soldiers this job he had assigned.

Holding the baby warmly swathed
Hills and valleys they steadily scaled,
Faced the ordeal of the chilling cold
And new problems that were untold.

Danger from robbers or animals wild
Didn't deter them despite their child,
In faith and hope they kept the secret
Until at dawn they entered Egypt.

3. After an Endless Wait

The earth was baptized, cleansed and rinsed,
By the flood for a spiritual makeover,
Sodom and Gomorrah weren't convinced
And God disliked their noxious behavior.

The twin cities in sulfur and fire end,
Noah gratefully welcomed the outcome,
Peace and renewal then began to blend,
Lot's rash wife had a statue become.

Israel got freedom but forgot the Divine,
Lost faith, direction and aimlessly wandered,
Their actions and feelings didn't align,
The good they owned had been squandered.

Their voice slipped into the ears of silence
Silence like darkness, just an abstraction,
An invisible, unbearable, unholy alliance,
A bottomless spiritual darkness of inaction.

The piercing rapture of the infant's voice
Slicing the air thick with the stink of sin
Proclaimed to the world to sing and rejoice,
Repair all damages and accept salvation.

The Savior had come after an endless wait
Amplifying the volume of the song of freedom
In a place and manner one didn't expect,
Angels blared out the advent of the kingdom.

4. I Baptized Him

I was baptizing in the Jordan River
Crowds had lined up along the beach
Suddenly Jesus stood as a sinner
Asking for baptism within my reach.

I told him it should be the other way
My need of baptism was far greater,
But he insisted, I had to obey,
A marvel occurred as he left the water.
Heaven opened its portal delighted,
I saw the Spirit of God descend,
Like a dove on him it alighted
And its grace all over extend.

I heard the voice of the Father resound
From the core of heaven it proclaimed:
"This is my Son, in love I'm bound
With him, indeed, I'm well pleased."

Jesus, though sinless, received baptism
For our sins and our sordid world,
On our earth he conferred his charism
A reborn life he wished to unfold.

Behold the Lamb of God', I shouted,
He's the Messiah, the Savior of the world
'He takes on him our sins' I insisted
'Follow him and give heed to his Word'.

'He comes after but was before me,
To undo his sandals I am unworthy,
He must increase and I'm to decrease
You be his disciples, obey his decrees'.

5. Feeding Five Thousand

Five barley loaves and two small fish,
A boy donated as dish,
Were enough for him to spread a treat
At his followers' meet.

Five thousand men, women and children
Ate to their satisfaction,
Twelve baskets of food in excess
Were saved in the process.

Jesus is big enough for any occasion,
However large your vision,
There's no obstacle you can't counter
For you're given his power.

This prefigures the Eucharistic Supper
He had wished to offer,
Bread and wine transformed to flesh and blood,
Our soul's nourishing food.

It is a lesson in faith and reliance
With our Lord in alliance,
Even when solutions seem impossible
He makes everything viable.

Bring your resources, no matter how small
Jesus will multiply all,
Compassion was the blossom of his heart
That helped to make the start.

6. A Memorable Wedding

For the guests it was a grand occasion
Stunning settings with servants to attend,
A captain on whom they could depend
And jars of water lined for ablution.

Food and drink was lavishly laid,
Wine was served and toast was raised,
Excellent taste of the wine was praised
Though its serving was unduly delayed.

He took time to turn water to wine,
"Fill the jars with water to the brim", he bade,
So to the town well, the bucket brigade
Went to haul gallons again and again.

Ever wondered why he delayed to act,
Didn't perform a miracle yet?
Why he made them struggle and sweat,
He wasn't in need of any help, in fact.

Man must first complete his given mission
Only then seek help his problems to solve,
Divinity then would intimately involve
Humanity's legacy for our salvation.

Jars to be filled to the brim implied
That man complete all he possibly could,
Then step back awhile and lo and behold
The astounding miracle he'd provide.

Short of wine meant a low in morals
Where righteousness had been drained,
Modern mindset produced a wasteland
That once brought man countless laurels.

Natural order which God had ordained,
The fabric of society, the family,
Lost its status and crumbled rapidly
Which unnatural unions explicitly profaned.

Man must struggle, even break his spine,
Till all the jars are filled to the brim
Gallons of water you may bring him
He'll still change it to genuine wine.

7. Jonah Flees from God

God is full of mercy and compassion
Regardless of ethnicity or religion,
He desires that everyone repent,
Forgives those who sincerely lament.

Jonah was sent to Nineveh to preach
A divine mission, the Lord's outreach,
He thought he could get away and hide
So he fled to the opposite side.

In Jonah our worst is seen magnified
We are guilty of disobedience and pride,
He boarded a ship to escape his task,
Went and fell asleep below the deck.

God sent a storm to rattle the ship,
Fear had the sailors in its firm grip,
Prayers to their gods didn't bring luck,
Then discerned a divine power at work.

They rolled the dice to find the guilty,
Jonah confessed he failed in his duty,
Requested that he be thrown in the sea,
The storm subsiding they didn't foresee.

God foiled Jonah's plan to break free
A watery tomb for him was his decree,
Cramped within the stomach of a fish
Roaming the sea bottom wasn't his wish.

The fish vomited Jonah on dry land
Back to the starting he hadn't planned,
Unhappy, though, he uttered a thanks,
Promised to obey and alter his stance.

8. The Transfiguration

We were the three of his inner circle
On our way to the Tabor pinnacle,
Walking with him in regular stride
For he was our leader and guide.

Suddenly his face turned dazzling bright,
And his clothes shone as white as light,
Revealing to us a glimpse of his glory,
In time he'd share the rest of the story.

Moses and Elijah of the ancient rite,
Many eventualities and failures despite,
Revealed the continuity of the salvific plan
God had been pursuing since time began.

The law giver and the prophet talked of his leaving,
They too had their own time of going,
The link of the Testaments, the New and the Old
In Jesus, the connecting bond to behold.

Peter suggested they build three cabins,
For such an occasion, as he imagines,
But the Father's words from the dense cloud
Was a clear command that echoed aloud.

The three disciples stooped in devotion
Listening to the words, "He is my son
In whom I'm pleased, to him you listen".
An experience they'd never have forgotten

9. The Temple of God

Extreme was his anger
Like a blazing fire,
When the house of prayer
Was made a trade center.

Bargaining and arguing
And dishonest dealing,
They traded their goods
From the temple courts.

He grabbed a long cord,
Took a step forward,
Made a strong whip
Their businesses to flip.

He drove out every animal
Both sheep and cattle,
Overturned the tables,
Scattered their shekels.

Severe was the warning
For his temple defiling,
Making a sacred space
Into a haggling place.

This makes us aware
Our body to declare
A temple of the Spirit,
With reverence to treat.

Restore its purity,
Its pristine beauty,
Dedicated for worship
And adore his Lordship.

10. Valley of Bones

Guided gently by an unseen hand
Ezekiel was led to a desolate land
Full of dry bones scattered about,
Which was indeed a shocking sight.

These were the remnants of a bygone race
Stripped of purpose in this forsaken place
His heart ached with the weight of the ages
Yearning for answers from different stages.

Can these bones be alive, he wondered,
A profound question that seemed absurd,
In that stillness echoed a command
Calling the bones to reassemble and stand.

The bones rattled and joined together
Sinew knitting them like a strong tether
Flesh coating their barren surface
With skin covering their entire phase.

The four winds breathed life and spirit
An army stood restored in form explicit,
Renewal is always within one's reach
Every end can be a beginning as such.

The landscape of despair moments ago
Was transformed into a resurrection show,
A display of divine power and promise
A message of renewal, hope and solace.

11. What His Star Reveals

Where is the star, where is its trail,
Where is the radiant glow ethereal
That led the Magi far from the East
To the new born Infant's feet?

In the glimmer of the sun kissed water,
In the glow of moths when the sky is darker,
In the sparkle of every innocent one's eyes,
You'll find the JOY of His star in disguise.

Look for it within the blisters of pain,
Examine the sweat of labor and strain,
Plunge into the scorching heat wave at noon,
The PAIN of His star has a comforting tune.
Inside the teardrops of every distraught,
And in every folded hands for support,

In the extended bowl of the lowly beggar,
You cannot ignore the DESPAIR of His star.

In the morning dew on the newly born leaf,
In the far pervading mist over the reef,
In the varied hues of Mother Nature
You'll surely find the HOPE of His star.

In the mighty rumbling roar of thunder,
That splits the edge of clouds asunder,
In the vibrancy of spirit in the youth concealed,
The awesome GLORY of His star is unveiled.

Take a gentle look at an expectant woman,
Peep in the sparrow's nest in the barn,
Or at the tangled web of the spider
You cannot miss out the LIFE of His star.

In the warm cuddle of a delighted mother,
In the lilting echo of a guileless laughter
In the embrace of the earth and the sky afar
You'll feel the enfolding LOVE of His star.

Track the trail of the star and on it rely,
Inhale its aroma as it passes by,
Listen to its song in the waft of the breeze,
A fruitful life of joy His star guarantees.

12. He Calms the Sea

Did you invite Jesus into your boat
When you ventured out into the sea,
The one that's your Sea of Galilee?
Did storms assail when you were afloat?

Did roaring waves with all their fury
Lash and toss you up and down
On the edge of the swirling water's crown,
Flooding your space in a mighty hurry?

Invite Jesus to the boat of your life,
Give Him charge to be at the helm,
He will take you far into the realm
Of peace and serenity devoid of strife.

Hands lifted towards the turbulent skies
He stills the storm and calms the seas,
Let not distraction destroy your peace
So alone on Jesus, focus your eyes.

13. Jesus Rides a Colt

The lord's in need of a colt yet untried
On which in splendor he wants to ride,
Like a monarch in grandeur and might
Through the city's roads in broad daylight.

On its back they spread a velvety sheet,
Unfurled their mantles on the main street,
Some even laid out branches of leaves
Cut from the palms that decked the fields.

Swaying branches they welcomed in glory
As he entered the gate triumphantly,
Waving branches they boldly acclaimed:
"Hosanna! Praise to the son of David."

Fickle by nature and feeble in mind
This motely rabble would soon turn blind
Demand Jesus be arrested and tried
And for treason should be crucified.

14. Laborers in the Vineyard

A landowner went out early one morn
For his vineyard to hire some men,
He agreed with them a denarius as pay
For the work they'd be doing all day.

At about nine he went out again
Met more standing idle in vain,
Again about noon and about three
He met some men lazy and free.

Sent them also to work in the field,
To pay them the proper wage he agreed,
Finally at five he met some more
Took them to the vineyard as he did before.

At the day's end the payment was made
All got the same amount, so they prayed
Those who worked longer should receive more
But the landowner showed them the door.

'We had agreed for one denarius a day
It's my money and I use it my way,
I haven't wronged you, so go away fast,
The last will be first, and the first, last'

15. Ten Lepers Were Healed

We were ten lepers calling out loud
'Unclean' and remained far from the crowd,
In humble demeanor we begged in unison
"Jesus, Master, pity our condition".

"Show yourselves to the priests," he urged,
On the way we felt our body was purged,
One of us returned and fell on his knees
Thanked and praised God and felt at ease.

'Were not ten cleansed? Where are the rest?
Only one returned, a Samaritan, an outcast,
Not even a part of God's own people!
Arise and go, your faith made you well.'
Jesus frequently crossed social boundaries
Accepted the marginalized, devoid of fineries,
Lepers were castoffs of the Jewish community
For they were sinners punished with

16. The Parable of the Two Sons

A man had two wonderful sons,
This is what to the first he spoke:
'Go to my vineyard and complete the work',
'No, I won't', the request he spurns;
But being sincere he went and did
What his father rightfully demanded.

To the other son he said the same
I'll definitely, sir,' the reply came,
But he didn't go, nor did he repent;
Who do you think obeyed the parent?
'Of course, the first son, all agree
For it's logical, as everyone can see'.

Sinners are entering heaven before us
For they experienced John's impulse
To follow his footsteps and his teaching,
And before the Lamb prostrate beseeching
Forever to be their leader and guide
And all the needed assistance provide.

The first son is like tax collectors
The Jewish outcasts, society's debtors,
Because they believed John the Baptist,

Who for repentance used to insist,
Accepted him despite initial rebellion
Before others they'll enter the heaven.

The leaders of Israel are the second son
Who claimed obedience, but had shun
Substance lack in their spirituality,
They had the leaves of activity
But not the fruit of repentance,
That's why for heaven they had no chance.

17. The Wicked Tenants

A landowner rented out his vineyard
And moved to a faraway land,
At harvest time he sent his servants
To collect his share from the tenants.

They seized his servants and beat,
Or stoned or killed in conceit,
At last he sent his own son
They'd respect, he was certain.

They killed him for the inheritance
Out of greed and arrogance,
So they met a wretched end
At the angry landowner's hand.
The stone the builders rejected
Has turned the cornerstone instead.
Everyone who falls on this stone
Into pieces will be broken.

18. The New Bethlehem

A cave where animals got shelter
You decided to make your home
Its unhealthy state you didn't alter
Diffused the cave with shalom.

You brought status and recognition,
Your presence changed this dank place
To a superior and noble dimension,
And transformed it a heavenly space.

A new Bethlehem is within me
Make worthy this cave so unholy,
The inn's loss was the shelter's gain,
If sin is rejected blessings obtain.

Reborn into this brand new manger
With the Lord in the tabernacle's chamber
An awesome privilege most gracious
I'm offered this treasure most precious.

I'll wrap you with warmth and love,
My whisper as the cooing of a dove,
I will sing you a sweet lullaby
And in your cuddle I will lie.

Let this manger remain lifelong
Beg our childhood you prolong
In worship your mercy we implore
With the Magi and the shepherds adore.

19. A Reed in the Wind

What did you search in the wild desert
A reed swayed by the wind's effort?
Or a man affected by popular trend
Of unstable nature trying to pretend?

What then did you go out to hear?
A voice crying out loud and clear
In a sterile and forlorn wasteland
That drew crowds to hear his demand?

Did you seek a man in silk apparel
Such as found in a royal castle?
Or a man wealthy and influential
Who could impact your potential?

Perhaps you went out to seek a prophet
The most recent one, John the Baptist,
Of whom you must've known or heard
The one your heart probably preferred.

Israel's leadership had grown corrupt,
God then promised a mighty prophet
Whose sanctified seat had been vacant,
And God's presence among them absent.

John deserved to be called a prophet,
To make the Messiah's way was his target,
Because he excelled in this profession,
The Messiah's harbinger by his direction.

A prophet was to foretell the future
And comment on man's fallen nature,
Warn people of the effect of their deeds
That their expectation often exceeds.

Prophets seek wilderness as a shelter
Prefer to accept the outdoor swelter
Than to submit to a worldly power
Who would kill their soul and devour.

20. The Storm Was Furious

The storm was furious and raging wild
Beating the water to raise high waves,
Tossing the boat in rhythmic tide
Rocking violently the man who saves.

He rested tranquilly despite the gale
Deep in the soothing arms of sleep,
Though the waters went on to assail
Until they woke him from slumber deep.

'Master, arise' in fear they cried
'We're in danger, don't you care?'
The ravaging waters heard him chide
And the storm to surface did not dare.

'O men of little faith why such fear
When I am with you there's no danger,
Seek me out whenever storms appear
In my presence no one is a stranger.

2. "WHAT IS TRUTH?" PILATE ASKED JESUS.

The answer can be found in the actions Jesus performed and from the comments he made at different occasions.

21. God's Immensity

God is majestic, august and immense
Vaster than his mighty universe,
It isn't static, its essence is certain,
He spreads the universe like a curtain.

His creation echoes in awesome wonder,
His voice rips the heavens asunder,
His majesty and power him magnify,
They send his lightning to zigzag the sky.

Hear the daunting roar of his thunder,
Horrid tsunamis pillage and plunder,
He rattles the earth in violent fury,
His whirlwind swirls the clouds unruly.

Trillions of galaxies and milky ways
Deck the universe to sing his praise,
King of all creation, the One Supreme,
Embellishes the earth with beauty extreme.

Variety of glorious colours and designs,
Mesmerizing tapestry of shapes and signs,
Aromatic fragrance enhancing vibrancy,
He embalms the world to assert his primacy.

Man is the ultimate emblem of his glory
Far beyond even every spiritual entity,
Thus the Almighty reveals his splendour,
Unveils his radiant and amazing grandeur.

22. On the Fabric of Creation

We are a part of God's creation
A marvelous experience profound,
To enjoy all forms of life and vocation,
Every emotion, sight and sound.

It is thrilling to flow with the stream
And leisurely meander relishing the fun,
Stand tall on peaks and loudly scream,
Salute the rising and setting sun.

With gay abandon, leap with ease
In the company of lambs and lions,
Fly and float on the wings of breeze,
Flutter and wave over dandelions.

Sail the oceans and with them blend,
Dance and swirl in the odor of flowers,
Fly with eagles to the farthest end,
Be drenched in the bounty of summer showers.

We are a burning tongue of flame
Kindling love and happiness around,
Let our stunning smile proclaim
The reason for living is worth and sound.

We're a glimmer in the star studded sky
Absorbed into the fabric of divinity,
An offering on the altar to certify
It's laid as the lifeline of humanity.

We are a dulcet note in the hymn
Angels sing to the Lord Divine,
An amen to the prayers offered to him
In thanksgiving to our God benign.

An emissary of God's chosen team
To proclaim aloud His unique missive,
Help realize the fruition of His dream,
In return, blessings in abundance, receive.

23. The Ultimate Sacrifice

We cannot unravel the mystery,
Nor guide anyone with mastery,
To fathom the depth of his sacrifice,
His ultimate self-giving has a price.

The Lord made a solemn vow
From the cross on Calvary's brow,
He made the essential oblation
A requisite for our salvation.

We may discuss with theologians,
Explore in hallowed grounds,
Or pour over erudite theses
To learn the sacredness of these.

We need to experience within
That to God we are akin,
When the sacred words are spoken
And his body and blood are taken.

He rests and melts on our tongue,
Permeates every part of our being,
We blend to evolve a fusion
Of divine and human vision.

Experience isn't a feeling
Instead a total revealing
Of God to man His presence
As he penetrates our elements.

One who enters the Mass
Must things mundane surpass
In spirit and in vital essence
With complete trust and reliance.

24. The Cosmic Temple

A cosmic temple is God's creation
Encasing all His panoramic vision,
Here he exhibits his masterpieces
And the contents of future releases.

Every element is simple and pure
Having its existence eternally secure,
Being in God's image and likeness
Bearing the mark of his divineness.

Man's dignity surges to the brim
When he belongs and becomes him,
Forming the mystical body of Jesus
Extended in time and space in us.

Take a leap of unwavering faith,
Brave the unknown that mars your path,
With just a dream and a heart full of hope
To find the truth, you've enough scope

25. Painted In Poetry

The canvas of creation portrays a tapestry
Of matter and form expressed in poetry,
Sound and silence twinkle unsubdued
Sight emerges to help blindness elude.

Rhyme and rhythm danced in ardent passion
Moving in tune with a vibrant fashion
Framing the scene as a permanent vision
To register in mind for ever a mission.

Light and shade blend forming a union
Of body and spirit in the realm of the One
Whose breath in whisper emits from the deep
To infuse His life in the human asleep

26. His Word Is Alive

The more we read the Holy Word
And deeply ponder in solitude,
The closer we approach the loving God
And obtain our famished soul's food.

When we hold the Holy Book
We cradle Jesus in our palms,
Its effects, we can't overlook
As His heart throbs within our arms.

Place it reverently against our hearts
Enshrined in our open hands,
Feel the soothing effect it imparts
By way of the peace and joy it commands.

His Word is dynamic and creative
Nourishes and nurtures our being,
Transforms every energy positive
And leads us to a life everlasting.

His Word is the torch, that lights the way,
The truth that reveals the cosmic Spirit
The eye of faith that thwarts our stray
And endows reason to recognize it.

The Word is love he paid with pain
So with love we accept and revere
Hoping His teachings with us remain,
And till death to them we shall adhere.

This awesome and unique encounter
With the word divine now made flesh,
Generates within us a vibrant wonder
Of a mystic love ever afresh.

His Word is delight to a weary ear,
An echo of love to a desolate heart,
A rainbow to remove a lurking fear,
And a switch to ignite a life to restart.

27. The Blood of the Lamb

The Israelites smeared their prime doorpost
And their lintels first and foremost,
With the blood the lamb they'd slaughtered
Before the angel of death appeared.

Moses ordered them to have this done
For that was the Lord's instruction,
So that they'd have no cause for alarm,
For the angel of death would not harm.

I didn't smear the blood of the lamb
For this practice was a cause of alarm,
But in devotion consumed its blood,
Purged from wickedness I felt loved.

The blood of the lamb is devoutly offered
To wash away sins and all their effects,
To compensate the harm we have suffered
Due to our offenses in all respects.

28. Do Not Enter Sodom

Do not enter the land of Sodom
It is the land, the symbol of evil,
For its ruler is vile as the Devil,
You'll be his slave without freedom.

Get out Sodom if you have entered,
Be baptized in the water of the Nile,
God will part the sea for a while
Rescue you from the land you ventured.

Sodom is a nation of idolatry,
Sensuality, error and sorcery,
Effeminacy and immorality,
Traps to accuse and frame you guilty.

Our spiritual Sodom needs a cleansing,
Against pestilence need erect fencing,
Actions and mindsets that are perverted
Should certainly be dislodged and aborted.

We visit Sodom when we indulge
In alliance unnatural and overtly divulge
And promote earnestly as normal trends,
That is abnormal and definitely offends.

A spiritual Sodom exists within us all
Within singles, families and nations,
We worship liberty in perverted posture,
And often promote the golden calf culture

29. Jesus' Second Coming

In anticipation we await his return
He keeps his promise, that is certain,
He may visit soon or he may delay
We need to be prepared every day.

His return is crucial for an ailing world
Steeped in wickedness and evil untold
Rampart in crime and moral decay
It's time for us to repent and pray.

His delay in return is an opportunity
To cleanse ourselves to mirror his purity
And ascend in glory on the escalator
To live in the abode of the Creator.

30. Let The Children Come

The Lord surveys the earth for souls
Prefers the delicate, young and pure,
Empowers them with crucial roles
To guide all elders to heaven secure.

He firmly demands that they be brought
Before his presence frequently,
To receive his blessings and to be taught
To love, obey and serve faithfully.

Children are angels before the Lord
Whose image they truly portray
He showers them with worthy reward
And protects them from going astray.

Guiltless, trusting and honest by nature
They reflect virtues of devotion and care,
His joyful company they love to treasure
And abundant happiness with him share.

They are like candles flickering and melting
Like flowers diffusing fragrance and wilting
Decking his altar in profound reverence,
Living their life following his preference.

31. He Fills Every Space

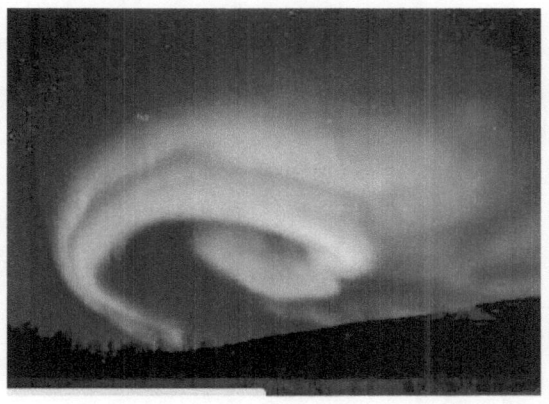

I see his love in the eyes of a blossom
Gazing at me as it sways in the wind,
The smile of its petals are truly awesome
Diffusing emotions unknown in kind.

His words echo in enthralling pulse
Like the buzz of the bee hummingbird,
Tiniest though, its influence unfurls
An ensign to assist even the weird.

His tears merge with the torrential rain
Without reducing in mass and flow,
That's how his endowments we may obtain
His largesse to the asking here below.

He pursued his mission with infinite thirst
Drawing to himself every kind of people,
Hi glory explodes like the thunder burst
And his mercy heals the sinful and feeble.

His sorrow is obvious, he cannot hide,
Its depth and magnitude we cannot gauge,
He wishes everyone in him abide
And become forever his mirror image.

32. The Chalice and The Womb

A receptacle, most sublime and sacred,
Worthy to contain His precious blood,
Priceless though made by human hands
Of matter sought by popular demands.

Its glittering inner reflects the innocence
Of the minister who raises it with reverence,
Whose eyes are divinely ordained to gaze
At the hallowed blood of the Lamb as he prays.

In chalice Christ offers as a libation
His precious blood for our salvation
To His Father in Heaven in expiation
For our offences as compensation.

If adorned in grace, is a female body
Whose womb proclaims a divine story
Which God has fashioned as a deific edifice,
For every womb is a potential chalice.

Each human body is sacred and revered,
Those in divine grace are most endeared,
The woman's womb cocoons a life to deliver
So it's an extension of God's creative power.

33. Broken And Scarred

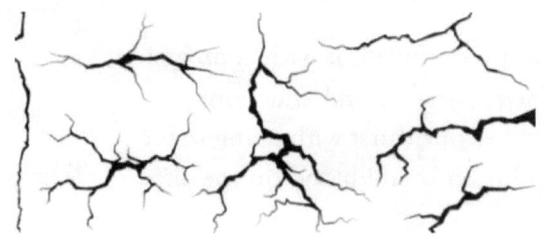

God often invades our comfort zone
Shakes us up and rattles every bone,
In the struggle for spiritual progress
Wants us to surrender all we possess.

He knows we are broken and scarred,
Messed up, frightened and scattered,
Full of stains that need to be purged
And unholy habits that casually surged.

We must unmask and reveal to the Lord
Hidden secrets in subconscious record,
The heavy burdens of worries and cares,
And approach Him humbly offering prayers.

Despite His majesty and immensity
He lowers Himself to our frugality,
Chips sharp edges to make them even
Our life's entire surface smoothen.

He winds up our wounds with compassion,
Tenderness, patience and affection,
He quenches our thirst with living water
Gives us his body and blood on the altar.

Why in the end then we can afford time
For everyone else, but not for Him?
We should be before Him on bended knee
Begging Him forgiveness and His mercy

34. A Voice in the Wilderness

I'm like the lion roaring in the wilds
Demanding all to attend to my calls.
A lonely voice that screams in the desert
To prepare a Highway and make it straight,
Every valley be raised and levelled
And every mountain lower settled.

Make the rough surface smooth and even,
Let rugged places have a plane pattern,
Speak to Jerusalem in tender demeanor
That Yahve has unfurled a unique banner
To lead them to prosperity and live in peace,
For he has accepted their worthy service.

God has called you to become the person,
For he created you to build a nation,
And do the things he designed you do,
He'll be a partner and walk along with you,
This process will be a spiritual journey
Leading you to heaven, though unworthy.

In His mercy, God calls you return
To be healed, cleansed and be forgiven,
The Lord is calling you to apply reason:
Though your sins are scarlet or crimson
He will make them pure white as snow
Restore your relationship and grace bestow

35. Salt of the Earth

When Christ said you be the salt of the earth
He meant you flavor the world with truth,
And splatter like salt his teachings about
That in every heart goodness may sprout.

To relish the savor of his precious food
Offered generously for everyone's good,
To spread his teachings to all corners
Offering comfort to repenting mourners.

The peace we exude, the joy we spread,
The ripple effects of kind words said,
Blessings showered on people in strife,
Are salt we spritz to energize their life.

The followers of Jesus had salt within,
Their life was flavored by his teachin',
It was to evoke peace and concern
In people who could share them in turn.

The salt in us helps us to stand erect
To confront a world that's vile and corrupt,
As salt preserves food from waste or decay
We're to persevere in times of dismay.

The salt of the earth is also each one
Though being simple, plane and common,
Can ignite a sparkle in dejected hearts
Revitalizing their insipid parts.

Salt stabilizes ingredients in food,
Enriches the color when it is cooked,
And enhances the flavor to suit the taste,
This is what we are called to imitate.

If the salt we sprinkle can create savor,
Transform every life by adding flavor,
And erase the stain tarnished by our fault,
Then we'll definitely be worth our salt.

36. His Masterpiece

I'm the rarest paragon of art
Crafted by the only expert,
His skill with brush and paint
Is awesome and most relevant.

He combines or contrasts colors
Lights and shadows as mirrors
Fashions the human entity
Resembling a revered deity.

Despite his varied creations
Not two of same dimensions,
He was the actual version
And we, a mere diversion.

37. The Human Soul

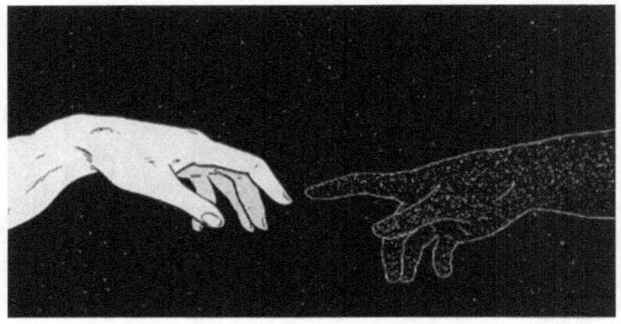

When we had been fashioned
And in our mother's womb laid
God breathed into our nostril,
And His breath formed our soul.

His gift, the immortal spirit,
His mirror image explicit,
With features he possessed
Freely we were vested.

The living entity that resides
In our body and guides,
Is a valid spiritual spark
Of the Supreme being's mark.

It is consciously aware
Of a transcendent power,
That provides the energy
To shield the soul from its enemy.

The soul partakes of the divine,
Enables us to think and reason,
Makes our nature benign,
With God's essence align.

The soul is spiritual and immortal,
Our life's vital principle,
To kill our soul there's no power,
It's ordained by the Creator.

38. Step Into the Sacred Space

Delve into the epochal messages straight
With an open mind and receptive spirit,
As we unravel the layers of grace,
Step into the heart of the sacred space.

God's in control with unwavering precision,
His love unfailing reveals his decision,
His words breathe life into our dreams,
Not on performance but on our themes.

We turn our trials into testimonies,
Our sorrow and pain into purposes,
Our hope is anchored in his promises,
They help us navigate life's realities.
Inhale the fragrance of his redemption
Offered freely to all through revelation.
Like a beacon piercing through darkness
Let his words be our safety harness.

39. Sacraments Have Power

The sacraments should be close to our side,
It's the most important factor to preside
Over our disordered and paralyzed being,
Like rays that penetrate us with healing.

The bleeding woman felt only his garment
To touch his body wasn't her intent,
Healing went out through his clothing
That's how sacraments graces bring.

Approach Jesus the eternal doctor
Show our wounds and ask for succor,
This divine physician will heal us in time
For services he won't charge a dime.

Gradual yet startling will be the healing
Without his assistance we can do nothing,
Healing is always about communion
About restoring what has been broken.

Receive not Jesus but become he,
He demands our heart, offer it free,
When he plunges in the sea of humanity
The waves travel to the ends of eternity.

Each sacrament gives us the special dignity
Of a profoundly true Jesus identity,
Stepping out of grace hardens our heart
So sacraments provide such life a restart.

When we pull a sheet over our face
We think we're safe from harmful rays,
Thus sacraments wrap us in their efficacy
Guard and defend us from the Devil's treachery.

40. If I Could Touch

If only I could touch
The hem of his garment!
What an awesome wish,
What a fine thought!
Its fulfilment would make
A world of difference.

The desire was simple
Didn't cost a penny,
The effort required
Was to stretch a little,
For help was at hand
In concealed assent.

A wishful thinking
Brings no reward,
This was a request
A result of a wish,
So it was granted,
The touch brought healing.

41. Yahweh's Chosen

The children of Israel
Yahweh's chosen people,
Were freed from bondage
Which was their heritage
In the Pharaoh's Egypt.

He led with deeds mighty
To a land of plenty
Flowing with milk and honey
Blessed them immensely,
Protected and loved them.

Despite failures repeated
He forgave the repented,
In their own land they settled
Made a nation grand,
And destroyed their enemies.

I too am a chosen,
Given faith and reason,
That our fathers had won
With trust and devotion,
In my heart it's a treasure.

A reason sufficient enough
To forego every rebuff,
And cherish this priceless belief
I'm God's anointed puff,
Blessed be the Lord our God.

42. Born in a Stable

He chose a stable in a cave to be born
Among animals cuddled in a pack,
A messy cave dank and forlorn,
Even basic essentials it did lack.

Man couldn't spare a room in the inn,
Nor be present when the Lord arrived
They couldn't find any accommodation
So they took shelter where animals survived.

No water or air clean and pure,
Cave walls were dripping with animal urine,
Floor full of filth that was hard to endure,
Yet they prepared a straw bed therein.

Mary laid her babe in a manger,
No man present, whom he came to save,
Dumb lowly animals welcomed the stranger
A unique privilege they seemed to deserve.

Poverty, negation and detachment he preferred,
A humble disposition lowly and modest
Was an important factor he'd favored,
That would alter his followers' mindset.

43. He Breathed Love into Life

Love to life is an intimate partner,
One cannot exist without the other,
It's an intense and profound bond
That's enjoyed on earth and beyond.

Divine Love is tender yet powerful
Constant, unconditional, and full,
Agape is the highest form of love
Bestowed upon us from heaven above.

God created man, his showpiece supreme,
Love got life when he breathed into him,
A love to be discerned, not to be seen,
A life to be felt and also seen.

Divine love is ardent and intense
Forgiving and with mercy immense,
The boundary of his love is without limit
Vast as the universe, ruled by the Spirit.

44. His Omnipresence

His love is revealed in the eyes of a child
His compassion in the breath of breeze
His care in the wrinkles of brows is implied
And his mercy to the contrite on their knees.

His words echo in enthralling cadence
In the whirring tone of the bee hummingbird
Though tiniest, it exerts much influence,
An ensign to lead the sad and defeated.

His tears flow in unending torrents
Nonstop without reducing its quantity
That's how generous his endowments
His largesse offered to the asking entity.

His face reflects a withering flower
Struggling to survive the onslaught of heat
His glory explodes to grant us the power
To confront the evil and force him to retreat.

His passion is veiled by the mask on his face
Disguising the harrowing pain he bore
Purging all those who wish to embrace
And holding on to him heavenward soar.

45. His Warning Thundered

"Woe to you Chorazin!
Woe to you, Bethsaida",
Was a warning against sin
And its consequences.

His words hung in the air
Heavy with deep meaning,
Gnawing their conscience
Like a relentless beast.

Now etched in their memory
Hope a tangible reality,
Pure unfiltered relief
Drew them to hope's threshold.

The gravity of the warning
Weighed heavy on the sinners
They repented, made amends
In sackcloth and ashes they dressed.

It, in deed, was a long shot
The only shot that was left,
Acceptance was proclaimed aloud
"Well-done my repented ones".

46. Be Generous

Ask for a flower
He gives you a garden,
Request for rain
Accept the deluge,

Beg for a beam
He floods you in light,
Appeal for a day more
He grants you long life.

Beseech forgiveness
He deletes your sins,
Pray for a child
He fills your cradle,

Plead for help
He sends you helpers,
God's generous to a fault
There is no doubt.

3. DOGMATIC TEACHINGS OF JESUS

From all the proclamations Jesus made to his apostles, to the followers and to the public in general and from the directives he placed before those who would follow his Gospel of Love, we have ample matter in this regard. A number of them are considered in this section

47. You are My Favorites

Come to me my angelic children
Who keep vigil at my alter,
You were with me in the garden
Watching I may not falter.

You are my favorite of all
You closely resemble my heart,
I'm happy to hear you call
Many are the favors I grant.

You're meek, humble and pure
Worthy to receive my grace,
Torrents of blessings I assure
If you come into my embrace.

Come to me a little closer
Tell me you love me and trust,
Speak to me of your fear
My outlook is tender and just.

Your fragrance reaches my throne
Heaven is in sheer ecstasy,
My shrine is for you alone,
I have made it your destiny.

O man erudite and still blind,
Unless you become like children
Humble, gentle and mild,
You'll never enter heaven.

48. Come to Me

When you feel lonely look at the cross
The Lord has both his arms outstretched,
"Come to me," He says with infinite force,
"You'll be cared for and feel refreshed."

When you're crushed under the weight of crime
And fail to move further despite effort,
Cling to His loving hand in time,
He will accept you and offer comfort.

When sins were repeated by fallen nature
When we'd reached the point lowest ever,
Betrayed him for a few pieces of silver
He didn't the final blow deliver.

If in such conditions you are delivered
There isn't a reason you won't be heard,
Anything more severe or grave be the deed
He'll always be there to help you proceed.

49. The Widow's Mite

They were watching a wave of folks
Drop their money in the treasury box,
Many rich people threw in large sums
The poor widow had just a few crumbs.

Calling his disciples Jesus observed:
The widow put in more, he declared,
Out of their excess most people gave
But she parted with all she could save.

A woman who lived in austerity
And who was in need of charity
Was a paragon of generosity,
And lived in truth and sincerity.

It isn't the amount of money given
It's the sacrifice involved therein,
It isn't the quantity of the offering
But the bounty showed in bestowing.

The tribute paid by the widow resounded
Louder than the wealth in the coffer landed,
The treasury proclaimed huge payments done
Only the widow's mites echoed from heaven.

God sees what man fails to observe,
He knows who does and doesn't deserve,
He saw the widow's gift worthy of praise,
Urged his men to follow her ways.

50. Blind Leads the Blind

When a blind leads another blind
They can only land in a ditch,
To find the right way they aren't inclined
For that's their unfortunate hitch.

When you look at the speck of dust
That your brother's eye displayed,
You will want him to place his trust
In your expertise to have it removed.

Your deceptive and devious nature
Hides the thick log in your own,
Though an obstacle by far greater
You prefer to avoid it or disown.

You hypocrite, first take your log out,
You'll then easily remove the speck
That you considered without doubt,
Keeping your brother's vision in check.

You are the ignorant who relies on another
Who is equally ignorant like you.
You follow him straight into disaster
To find you receiving what's your due.

51. The Power of His Blood

The blood of Christ is a divine weapon
Offered as a price for our salvation,
The Eucharistic drink to refresh our souls
From every disease, Protects and controls.

The blood on the doorpost saved the Israelite
It was the power in the blood of Christ
When people accept Christ as their potion
They're sure to receive a "blood transfusion".

From evil, danger and attack of the enemy
It provides refuge, healing and harmony,
When we're washed in the Lamb's saving blood
We are a cleansed from every dirt and purified.

It's a stream of mercy, refuge and healing,
Victor over demons, solace of the dying,
Relief in sorrow, hope of the penitent,
Courage and strength of the despondent.

It cleanses the stain of Adam's sin.
Redeems mankind with grace within,
We are justified, forgiven and redeemed,
And from God's wrath we are screened.

If our garments are stained with sin
Have them washed in His blood for cleansin',
They will turn spotless and white as snow
And our soul will possess a perennial glow.

Drink His blood and be spiritually alive
Be reclaimed from our foes and survive,
Any part of our life cut off from His being
Is like a fountain dried up or dying.

52. The Withered Arm

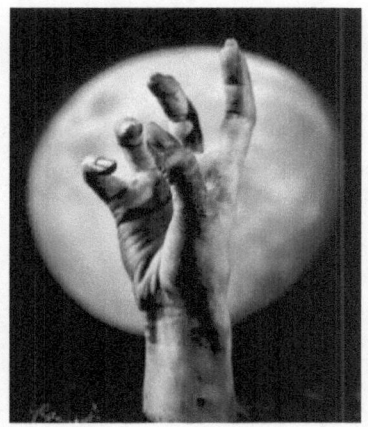

'Stretch out your hand', the order came
From the man who just entered,
He knew the Pharisees would surely blame
So in advance his regret he rendered.

He held out his withered hand in fear
In answer to the Rabbi's request,
But waited anxiously his mind unclear
What if the Pharisees protest?

Jesus looked about seeking approval
But saw their eyes of reproach,
He seemed facing an unholy tribunal
Who wouldn't permit him preach.

He didn't come here to seek their consent
But to reveal his mission,
Present before them the means to repent
And follow his new vision.

Adam by plucking the forbidden fruit
Tied up the hands of man
Stretching his hands Christ solved the dispute
Restored the arm and its tan.

53. Take My Yoke Upon You

Lay down the burden you now carry
Take a little rest,
Hold this, my yoke, do not tarry,
You will find it the best.

Lay it on your weary shoulder
It's sure easy and light,
Follow me then, be a little bolder
Your path will shine bright.

Heavy the weight that falls your way
Asking you to drag it along,
Despite its outlook ugly and gray
It won't last that long.

You'll experience satisfaction
When you reach your goal,
The reward for your sincere action
Will benefit your soul.

54. A Theocentric Treasure

When we enter a Catholic shrine
We are entering Jesus Christ,
Kneeling before the Sacred Host
By radiation therapy we outshine.

Adoration is a sign of devotion
A homage of the spirit paid to the King,
In the Consecrated Host we bring
The human and divine as our potion.

No voice is heard, just a whisper,
Like liquid love it pours over us
Divinizing our existence thus,
Making our life a theocentric treasure.

This sacramental bread is the essence
That ardently draws us to Jesus,
Gently transforms and stimulates us
To bask in the warmth of his real presence.

In silent reverie and deep reflection
We enter into a spiritual union,
Snuggle up to him and form a fusion
A unity of God and his creation.

55. Follow Me

My booth was tucked in heart of the city
Where I served with the tax committee,
Long were the queues before my counter,
Dealing with tax payers is an encounter.

I was in my booth sitting alone
Suddenly emerged this person unknown,
Startled I stared in shock and dismay
'Follow me' said he and went on his way.

I felt an inviting magnetic pull,
I couldn't resist, my senses went dull,
On impulse I followed him into his tent,
Then I knew I felt an interior bent.

Our meeting called for a celebration
To share the much needed relaxation,
The best of food served with vintage wine
Made the occasion simply divine.

The Pharisees accused the Master in rage
'A prophet shouldn't with sinners engage,
You create a scandal when you align
With men who willfully our image malign'.

'Only the sick need a doctor' he said,
And for a sinner true regret needed,
Here I am for the sick and the sinner
The healthy and well, need no healer'.

56. Celebrate The Passover

"Come with me to the upper room
Let us celebrate the Passover feast,
Though clean, yet I wash your feet
To get you set for the ultimate treat".

'You mustn't do Lord, it's so humbling,
You are our Rabi and we're just pupils,
Wrapped in defects and moral scruples,
Blow flagrantly our faults through bugles'.

"Here is the choicest meal I've spread
My broken body and my blood too,
Accept as treasures of utmost value
Consume them and life eternal pursue.

"Do it for others for they too are in need
Let my self-offering be an example
You too must follow and don my mantle
Become me and proclaim my preamble".

57. Be Holy as I am Holy

Attaining holiness is not an option
In the divine strategy it's a decision,
We can harness the Lord's holiness
To transform and upgrade our lowliness.

God demands his consuming fire
Should engulf us and mold every desire,
Without destroying he makes us immortal,
And welcomes us at his sublime portal.

God had set the standard so lofty,
None can reach it, for we are faulty,
It was a recipe for despair and fear
So Jesus came to help us adhere.

Sin is a spiritual suicide for God,
When in sin, we are a mere fraud,
God is closer than we to our selves
He beckons us to where he dwells.

58. A Profound Mystery

The ground wheat is transformed to bread
And crushed grapes, a wholesome drink
When as votive offering I spread
On the altar of oblation before our King.

The paten holds the bread of wheat
The chalice carries the purest wine
When the consecration prayer is complete
We have his flesh and blood divine.

On our tongue He melts and dissolves
Permeates our entire essence
Our unworthiness he absolves
And keeps us always in his presence.

Our hearts ardently throb in unison
And in a mystic alliance intertwine,
Never separating, always as one,
In form and essence we align.

It's always a profound mystery
That holy God and sinful man
Should fuse as one genetically,
And make a unity as only God can.

59. Revealed to Children

The Father had a plan in mind
That he wanted to share,
With the wise he wasn't inclined
For they wouldn't much care.

So he revealed it to children
Whose mind could easily grasp,
For they had high acumen,
Could keep it in protective wrap.

Their heart is the right receptacle
That can securely conceal,
When needed it is retrievable
And can swiftly reveal.

Be like children in mind
Age shouldn't interfere,
Pure and trusting in kind
And to His laws adhere.

60. Hold on to His Cross

Hold on firmly to the cross of Christ
Whenever you are assailed by doubt,
The only thing that matters after all
Is the truth you'll never falter or fall.

Things we prioritize in life and sought
Will become a distant afterthought,
Things we own become insignificant
If the cross isn't deemed magnificent.

People look at everything but not at the cross
They'd prefer to see beauty and gloss,
Your belief in the cross you must enforce
And boast in the cross and shout in applause.

The world watches you and your goodness
But hesitant to accept you as a witness
Hardened sinners dare not confront
The Gospel message that's direct and blunt.

If you think you deserve heaven
And heaven isn't heaven, unless you're in,
You're like the Pharisee with righteousness,
Unlike the publican exposing his abjectness.

Hold on to the cross when death's at the door
Request like a child your worth to restore,
A child that boasts in the cross of Christ
Can remain chaste all day and all night.

God has made an appointment for each
One that enables us for death to beseech,
When our chance comes we can discern
How we can boast in the cross in turn

61. A Tree and Its Fruits

False prophets in sheep's attire
Are seen as they secretly conspire,
Focused to misguide every gullible
In ways that appear believable.

Inwardly they are ravening wolves,
Death and ruin their goal involves,
A corrupt tree grows only rotten fruits
And the pure atmosphere it pollutes.

Every tree that bears inferior fruits
Should be pulled out by its roots,
Flunk into the sea of scorching flames
As a penalty for its illegal claims.

People are like trees, good or evil,
Good men will always possess good will,
So do evil men steeped in vileness
Live in wickedness and lawlessness.

If the source of the evidence itself is tainted
Anything got from it is also infected,
If a man's behavior appears noxious,
At heart he must certainly be callous

62. Woe to You

Passing through an ancient cemetery
I came across some graves well decked,
What Jesus had said about the Pharisee
Instantly leaped into my mind unchecked.

They were hypocrites, whitewashed tombs
Which looked beautiful from the outside,
Painted and polished in fresh costumes,
But were unclean with dead man's bones.

The Pharisees appeared of the same breed
Righteous and faithful on the outside,
But from the inside full of greed,
Hypocrisy, wickedness and pride.

Pondering silently on an old tomb,
What it contains unseen and unknown,
I thought a Pharisee hid in its womb
His remains guarded by a painted stone.

63. Ten Virgins

Ten virgins await the bridegroom's arrival
Chosen to escort him to his wedding ritual,
The five wise had oil in their lantern,
Their sacred duty they didn't abandon.

All the ten virgins at the groom's delay
Went off to sleep in drowsy dismay,
But soon were alerted in readiness stay
The groom and courtiers were on the way.

The foolish had no oil and asked from the wise
Who refused outright to make compromise,
Lest their supply run short when they're in need
Advised the foolish to the market proceed.

While they were away the bridegroom arrived,
The wise went in and the doors were secured
The foolish cried out, 'Open the door',
Although they knew what was in store.

"Certainly I tell you, I don't know you."
The groom's emphatic reply came through.
Watch out hence, for you know not the hour,
Nor the day when the Lord comes in power.

64. The Most Precious Love

A love that's precious and tender,
Never ending in splendor,
Steadfast, pure and profound,
Only in God can be found.

His love is gracious and faithful,
Boundless as the sky it's eternal,
Unchanging, caring and forgiving
Is seen in our pain and suffering.

God's love is unfailing and merciful,
His agape love is unconditional,
Despite our sins and failure
And most offensive behavior.

Love is a part of His character,
A salient mark of our protector,
Never will it fade or vanish
And the offer is always lavish.

65. We Let Down the Net

We struggled all night casting our net
That brought only distress and regret,
Though we ventured away from the shore
We failed and returned our effort to deplore.

"Let down your net into the deep,
A large enclosure let it sweep,
These are unchartered territories
That could reveal rare mysteries".

A repaired and redeemed net is cast
Into an ocean serene and vast,
The time was ideal for a good catch
Though we expected a possible mismatch.

The net was pulled towards the boat
Filled with bubbling life afloat
In shock and awe the neighbors helped
For such a catch we hadn't expected.

66. Call to Holiness

When we take our first step to sanctity
It's the start of a long strenuous journey,
Through ups and downs we may traverse
And often encounter situations averse.

God props us up where we least expect
That's unfamiliar and uneasy to accept,
We must walk down the road of prayer
For without that there's no getting there.

We could take the trail transcendental
Unwrap the mysteries concealed by veil
Or choose a track that's easy to tread
And proceed at our own pace instead.

Whatever be the choice we make
Will be to become holy for His sake,
For he called us purely to this end
So there's no reason for us to pretend.

Our ears attuned to celestial music
And our soul enthralled and ecstatic
We proceed steadily emitting rays
From sparks of truth and love's blaze.

Let the delightful laughter of our soul
And the rapturous hymns sung to extol
Gift-wrapped in one throbbing cadence
Resound as echo in His presence.

So shall our holiness blend and unite
With the unique form of a divine rite
Offered in oblation to the Most Holy
And be redeemed and crowned in glory.

67. Lay Your Hands

Place your hand on my head
With heavenly blessing,
Remove the evil of dread
I've been experiencing.

Let your spirit enter
To claim me your own,
Be my soul's mentor
My spirit's heavenly throne.

Let evil assets discard
Free me once again,
And wickedness be barred
At the entrance detain.

So shall my spirit rejoice
And ever endeavor
To proclaim in loud voice
Yours now and forever.

68. He Heard Me Call

He heard me call out loud
From deep within my heart,
The reply pierced the cloud
Which split my soul apart.

Eloquent was its impact
Resonated within my depth,
Stirred up the shallow tract
To come to light from stealth.

Fear knocked at my heart,
I was disconcerted,
Trust provided the start,
Hope assistance asserted.

My response was spontaneous
No hesitation persisted,
Smoothly flowed out harmonious
That heaven accepted.

69. Harsh Reminders

Some of the hardest moments in life
We had been through but left behind,
Come around to stab us like a knife
The harsh forgotten facts to remind.

Often at death bed they announce
To rattle our conscience from it depth,
Urging earnestly its sins renounce
As it approaches its final breath.

Fear and tension then mar our horizon
Uncertain who to turn for assistance,
Confront not this new situation
But fall at the feet of the Merciful Prince.

70. Who is the Greatest

Everyone wants to be greater than others
In position, status and other matters,
So too the sons of thunder wanted
As their mother had wisely demanded.

The two seats on the left and the right
Of their Master's throne, despite
Standing in queue ten more others,
Should be reserved for the two brothers.

The gravity of their request unaware
To drink his cup, ready they were,
But the two seats had been prepared
By his Father and in advance reserved.

Whoever wants to be the first and great
Must be a slave and his ego deflate,
The Son of Man didn't come to be served
But have his life as a ransom offered.

71. If Jesus is Lost

If Jesus is lost
Everything is lost,
You're a wreck
Your edifice crumbles
You don't exist,
Your life is swallowed
By a somber void.

Wriggling in the womb
Of dark oblivion
Fear and despair
Dog your trail.
Your dreams and goals
Lost track and meaning,
Vague is your vision.

Search and you'll find
'Twas his injunction,
No life without him
For life is the gift
Bestowed by Jesus,
Search for the Lord
And you'll find peace.

72. The Need to Expiate

He needed to expiate a hidden sin
That was groaning and gnawing within,
His effort to commence the process again
Fell through before he could even begin.

His conscience, a cactus of titanic size,
Its needles offered him means to chastise,
His blood oozing out was no surprise,
And its wetness he didn't despise.

He prayed and fasted hoping to gain
The pardon he had been seeking in vain,
And rid his mind of excessive strain,
And a calm and peaceful status attain.

73. Who's My Mother

Shared faith verily outweighs kinship,
But our life's foremost relationship
Is to live in harmony with our God
And understand his eternal Word.

Even the strongest family ties
At conception when we unite implies
To God we belong in the true sense,
Before we're allied to anyone else.

Jesus' mother and relations came
Wanting to have their affinity claim,
Even though the crowd hindered their entry
He didn't go out immediately.

Stretching forth his hands at his followers:
'Behold my mother and my brothers!
Whoever does the will of my Father
Is truly my mother, sister and brother'.

74. Atrocious Indictment

Jesus sprayed a hail of bullets
Of startling charges on their rant,
Teachers of the law from their pulpits
And Pharisees for their self-righteous chant.

His anger blazed their ghetto mindset:
They refuse outright to enter heaven,
And prevent others with ruthless threat
If an iota of the law was broken.

Rigidity is their supreme protector
Loaded with hypocrisy and deceit,
External adherence to the law in letter
Far exceeds its observance in spirit.

They feign sanctity and moral standards,
Pretend to perform as expected of them,
Burden the gullible with trivial demands,
Any default or weakness they condemn.

The awesome truth revealed in the Word
Must compel our egotism to relinquish,
Will his finger indict our record
And constrain us to prostrate in anguish?

"Life was my foremost precious gift
You wasted it on the trivial and odious,
I gave you love but you profaned it
And made it base and felonious.

"A large and beautiful house you had
You closed yourself in, shut others off,
You ill-spent your wealth, it was quite sad!
Treated the needy with disdain and scoff.

"Your knowledge, intellect and your youth
Were some roadshow of pride and conceit,
You employed wisdom to twist the truth
And the innocent and trusting to outwit.

"Your physical strength and mental prowess
Oppressed the helpless and the downtrodden.
Willfully tampered to blunt your conscience
Disfigured its essence and kept it hidden.

"These accusations predict your fate
So staunchly resolve to replace the woes
Make amends to reclaim your state
With a firm hand cudgel your foes."

75. Net Full of Fish

The net was full and ready to burst
With fish galore,
The fishermen drew the net aghast
To the crowded shore.

They sat by this unexpected catch
Sorted out the best,
Decided them to the market dispatch
A fitting way to invest.

The small and the strange were discarded
They had no value,
So flung them back to the sea unrecorded,
Couldn't generate revenue.

Thus be the state at the end of days,
The angels to do the sorting,
The wicked be thrown to the raging blaze
The good, receive his blessing.

76. New Wine in Old Wineskins

The new wine needs a fresh new skin
Space for fermenting and expansion,
Shouldn't be brittle or inflexible
For the bottle's ruin is inevitable.

Putting new wine into old wineskin
Often causes explosion within,
The wine that's spilled can't be redeemed
When your friends are in urgent need.

Old skins are like the Pharisees' rules
Stored as reminders and used as tools,
A means to enforce their rigorous laws
On gullible public because of their flaws.

Pharisees are like the old wineskins
Store rooms for old laws and traditions,
Averse to changes and rigid in their views
Despite the benefits the new law pursues.

77. A Wedding Invitation

A wedding banquet is on the cards
And I'm invited to attend,
But I must show love and regards
Lest my new wife, I offend.

I've bought a farm I must check
And the new oxen feed,
So this invite I have to reject
And should pay no heed.

The furious king rejected the invited
Welcomed all the commoners,
With royal food they were provided
As for high ranking foreigners.

Strictly enforced the royal dress code
Formal and fitting the event,
Any deviation from the princely mode
Was banned to the fullest extent.

A man in the crowd was sent to exile
For his informal attire,
If sanctity of the event, guests defile,
They're compelled to retire.

78. Is Divorce Lawful

'I want to divorce my wife',
'The law says you can't',
'But I have reasons of strife
About her defiant rant'.

'No reason is valid for males
To divorce their rightful females,
For God had made them both
The two are one by oath'.

'But Moses allowed divorce
A written proof to enforce',
'Because their hearts were hard
And with evil intent scarred'.

If we divorce and remarry
We'll be committing adultery,
Then it's better to stay single
And forego the joys of mingle.

79. Hold on to My Hand

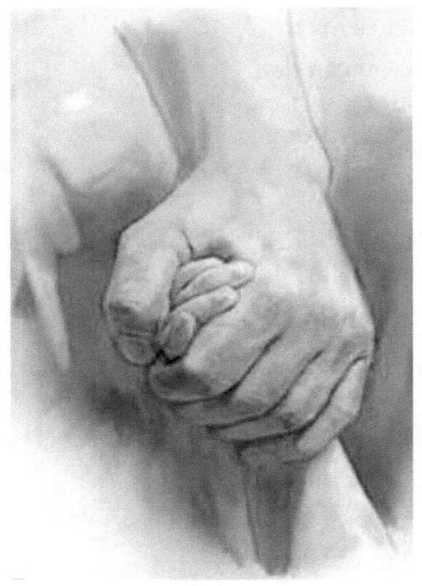

Our God is the Alpha and the Omega
Who embraces a mysterious aura,
He's in the business of doing the unexpected
When our soul is with wounds inflicted.

He meets us at the height of our pain,
Surprising us with the grace to attain
And transform our spiritual perspective
Into accomplishments most effective.

His promise of a divine intervention
Can change everything with right intention,
The path ahead may seem daunting and scary
Obscured by the shadows of uncertainty.

"I'm making a way in the wilderness
And streams for you in the waste's vastness,
Hold on to my hand extended to lead you
Hesitate not, have faith firm and true".

80. They Questioned Jesus

John's disciples and the Pharisees
Questioned Jesus about Fasting,
'How come despite the decrease
Your men are observed feasting'?

'Can guests of the bridegroom fast
When he's in their midst'?
'This is in stark contrast
To what you wish to insist'.

Fasting reveals the hunger,
An inner longing for God,
Whose coming in splendor
Had been long foretold.

Fasting is self-control that purges
A heart reeling in its plight,
A spiritual rule of the ages,
That assists a heart in contrite.

Fasting depicts a parting
Between the bride and the groom,
When in times of their meeting
Everything will joy assume.

When from Jesus they're apart
That's when they will fast,
If from this way we depart
It negates our longing for Christ.

81. *I'm Not Here for Peace*

You are mistaken oh man of Law
Projecting always a deceptive show,
Pool in nothing for the common good
Being a venomous viper's brood.

I haven't come here to bring you peace,
Nor I intent your importance increase,
I have come mainly to create division,
Bring about conflict and confusion.

You will see people cross one another,
Parents and children fighting each other,
Until they seek the peace only I give
Peace you would enjoy when

82. Searching for Jesus

It was at the Passover feast
When Jesus appeared lost,
Their search proved futile
For the Rabbis had him awhile.

Angst afflicted the parents,
Their agony flowed in torrents,
This is the standard result
When you know Jesus is lost.

The men failed to discern
To Emmaus at their return,
Until he broke the bread
Before he disappeared.

Magdalene asked to be given
Her master's body in person,
But Jesus she failed to proclaim
Until he called out her name.

When Jesus is out of our sight
Or most wanting him despite
Or not discerning his facets
Can cause the loss of our assets.

83. The Eye of a Needle

He was earnest in giving the lesson:
It's hard for the rich to enter heaven,
It is as impossible as for a camel
To enter through the eye of a needle.

Wealth in abundance cloud their value
Time is limited and effort ne'er begins,
The only urge is to grab assets new
Till they realize they're steeped in sins.

None can be saved but only who repent,
And who willingly leave everything
To follow Jesus and life to him extent,
To receive infinite glory and blessing.

The Lord will sit on his glorious throne,
You will sit beside him on either side
Judging the tribes of Israel, your own,
To welcome the worthy by you reside.

84. He Came to the Rescue

He came to rescue us from crime's ravages
From the resulting death for all eternity,
To sharpen our awareness of the reality
Of the final judgment and its damages.

We shouldn't spend our life in the company
Of the evil one, for that isn't his due,
Fortify our resistance and grow in virtue
And participate in His divine symphony.

He invites us to be drawn into his passion
And enter his humanity in ardent devotion,
His divinity that he shares with his father
He offers us lovingly as a prestigious honor.

85. Your Nourishing Food

If I'm eighty and more
And still have health in store
It's been only your food,
Your living flesh and blood.

I seldom missed your treat
Even in Covid's heat
It was a gracious priest
Who helped me in discreet.

Missing you two months I wept
There wasn't any way except
Online the sacrifice celebrate
Unable your meal to partake.

Daily Mass and communion
Regular monthly Confession
Adoration of Blessed Sacrament
Are means that help me repent.

These days I'm quite concerned
Sugar and pressure I've discerned
Fluctuate in abnormal manner
Making life's flow irregular.

I consult my physician
In his basement shrine
As I prostrated and cry
He tells me I shouldn't worry.

86. The Vital Principle

All living humans enshrine a soul,
Spiritual in essence it can control
Every formal response and reaction
And the cosmic consciousness in man.

The soul is the most vital principle,
Infuses life and makes us functional,
Creates awareness of the value of life,
And its purpose, and meaning of strife.

The essence conferred on humanity
Is a miracle performed by his divinity,
Its spiritual form is the most essential
Which is often the most influential.

Finding immersed in an ecstatic vision
Our soul ascends the height of cognition,
When soul and body are forged in fusion
It erases the slim line of demarcation.

87. The Weed in the Crop

I had sowed the best of seeds
In my freshly prepared farm,
To my grief I found also weeds
This sight was a cause for alarm.

I knew it was my enemy's act
That was committed in the dark,
Envy had a tremendous impact
That in his heart lit the spark.

I didn't think it wise to uproot
Lest with the darnel, crops too perish,
Their mingling growth I didn't dispute
So this new bond they could cherish.

I shall deal with the mature darnel
When I send men to reap the harvest,
I'll sort them out and burn them in Hell,
And for crops my barn is the best.

88. Pray Without Ceasing

Prayer is being one with God,
What you do or think or say
Can be the ideal way to pray
And adore and worship the Divine Lord.

Prayer is surely the primary axis
On which every life should revolve,
It is the orbit you shouldn't miss
For it's from there you must evolve.

Prayer is the root of all existence,
The gentle breeze that ever unveils

God's concealed countenance,
To admit his will ever prevails.

Prayer penetrates every fence,
Can soften a hardened heart,
Fortify a crumbling defence,
And hope and trust greatly impart.

Prayer is like Jacob's ladder
That bridges man and his God,
With humble and honest candour
Can ascend on his own accord.

You need to empty all pain and grief,
Struggles, failures, loss and flaws,
Then extent your hands for relief,
You won't miss His praise and applause.

4. BIBLICAL PERSONALITIES

As in every event, space and time we come across extraordinary persons and ordinary persons performing extraordinary feats when confronting unexpected situations, we too have wonderful people in our Sacred Scriptures. They are models for us to emulate, or imitate the least. They stand out as giants of virtues, valor, and accomplishments beyond our ability or imagination. Here we delve into the lives of some of them.

89. Hail My Lady

'Hail my lady, virgin most pure,
Rejoice, with God you've found favor,
In your womb you'll conceive a son,
To bring forth for us the Redeeming One.

'The Lord will give him King David's throne,
This kingdom will his progeny own,
Their reign in power will never cease,
Until their God they dare displease.

'How can this be for I'm a virgin
And I have not been with any man?'
Troubled at heart Mary replied
Wondering what this message implied.

'The Spirit of the Lord will descend with grace
Overshadow your hallowed space,
You will then feel a stirring within
The sacred womb where life's to begin'.

'Here am I your servant, my Lord,
Let it be done to me according to your word'.
At these her words creation exulted,
For salvation had been long awaited.

90. The Carpenter's Son

'Hold on, I say, who is this man,
Isn't he the carpenter's son?
Joseph and Mary are our neighbors
So are his sisters and brothers.

'Where did he get such unusual wisdom
To speak to us with authority?
The power and talent and manner to perform
Deeds and wonders with maturity'?

'Why take offence at what I've declared
Wasn't it right and proper?

To accept truth your ego isn't prepared
For it's too odious a matter.

'You promote vile views and with them agree
The rest you prefer to disown,
A prophet isn't honored in his country
Nor accepted by his own'.

91. John the Baptist

No man born of a woman
Is greater than the Baptist John,
He lived all life in the desert
Clad in camel's hair and belt,
Ate locusts and wild honey,
A celibate ascetic was he.

Repent, be baptized he declared,
Prepare the Lord's way, he blared,
You too, brood of vipers
Forget your Jewish ancestors,
Produce fruit with repentance,
Own the Promised Land, be not tenants.

The axe is laid to the root,
The tree that bears no fruit
Be cut and flung in the fire,
To burn there forever.'
The voice in the wilderness said
And made sure everyone heard.

Someone powerful is on his way
He must increase and I stay,
His sandals to untie unworthy
Your awaited Messiah is he,
The new Elijah, the prophet,
In whose footsteps, a guest.

People in need of a savior
With Elijah had an encounter,
Even though he was beheaded
When King Herod had ordered,
John pointed to the Lamb of God,
'Follow him', was his last word.

92. Two Expectant Mothers

These two women of impeccable nature
Are on their way to motherhood,
One is of simple and delicate feature,
Humble with love imbued.

One is secluded from public gaze
Outside her obscure village,
The other, an elderly in childless disgrace,
Though born of noble lineage.

An object of everyone's ridicule and scorn
In trust to God she clings,
There's an evil spell, they discern,
On her this sterility brings.

Their affinity is a powerful tie,
Their conception is mysterious
No human wisdom can ever justify,
The Spirit's influence is obvious.

They heard the news in awe and wonder
The heavenly messenger conveyed,
They felt privileged to wholly surrender
For God's acceptance they prayed.

They are to play some pivotal roles
In the history of redemption,
In God's eternal plan for souls
Offered with love and affection.

93. The Good Shepherd

He is the Good Shepherd of the flock,
Sheep is his favorite of all livestock,
Lavishes love and care in abundance
To give his life he has no reluctance.

Knows every sheep, even by name,
Strong or weak, healthy or lame,
They know his voice even from distance,
At his call they around him prance.

There are no fences for their protection
So leads them to the sheepfold direction,
They do not scatter but huddle in one place
Away from others that occupy this space.

There's no gate at the sheepfold entrance
So he lies there to check unwanted presence,
And keeps guard against wolves and thieves
Who kill or steal or commit other extremes.

He opens the sheepfold early in the morning
Calls out each name without any warning,
Gently leads them to fresh green pastures
And for a drink to some refreshing waters.

Wandering across the trackless land
One could lose way or be left behind,
He leaves the rest and goes in pursuit
Brings it home on his shoulder aloft.

Pastors are shepherds of their faithful,
Who protect and defend each individual,
Drenched in the smell of their own sheep
Should aspire to provide moral upkeep.

94. My Guardian Angel

My angel is unique and special,
His love and protection crucial,
He affirms to him I belong,
Under his wings I'm strong,

Gentle and calm by nature,
Holiness, his prime feature,
Contemplates God's face,
And obtains for me His grace.

His love hasn't start or end
From birth to death a friend,
You may provoke or hurt
His love he'll always assert.

Day and night he's near
A protector and a messenger,
He never abandons me,
For me he's God's trustee.

95. Simeon the Prophet

After an endless futile rest
Into my extended arms he came,
Oh that moment highly blest
Held my breath, I couldn't exclaim.

Bathed in emotions of hope and wait,
For centuries men in anxious thirst
His sudden arrival didn't anticipate
But his joy and good will, on me burst.

As Mary and Joseph revealed the infant
Grace exceeding wrapped me round,
Filled with the Spirit in that instant
The prophecy I predicted was profound.

Centuries we waited in expectation,
People arrived and left the world,
In vain they held their aspiration
Bereft of the joy of his comforting Word.

Ann and I were the privileged people
Chosen to proclaim his timely advent,
His mission was to rescue the feeble
Their death and damnation prevent.

God kept his word, I saw the Redeemer,
It's time I went, so I told his parents
Pain would alter his gentle demeanor
Sorrow would flood their hearts in torrents.

96. Daughter of Phanuel

Anna lost her spouse at a young age,
Since then she wrote her story on a page
In the book of seclusion and self-sacrifice,
Living in the temple, offering her service.

She led a life of silent negation
Serving the Lord with intense passion,
Singing praises or praying in silence,
Reading Scripture to grasp its essence.

Always within the confines of the temple,
Away from people, her life was simple,
Delving deep into the core of heaven
Fasting and pleading for sins forgiven.

Lighting candles and burning incense,
Kneeling in prayer in divine presence,
Decking the altar with flowers of fragrance,
Reciting Psalms she paid obeisance.

Prophetess of God, daughter of Phanuel,
Awaited the arrival of Emmanuel,
Day and night she worshipped and prayed
To see the Messiah when he arrived.

On her mission she was persistent
Always be focused was her intent,
She's the paradigm of resolute waiting
Even when the delay seemed unending.

97. Joseph the Just

Emerging from a background hidden and silent,
Born in a dynasty of royal heritage,
Stands out a carpenter from Nazareth village
As a beacon of hope for a world noncompliant.

Gleaning his life reveals a man of modesty
Gentle in manner, self-effacing by nature,
Profound in holiness, reverential in feature,
Obeying God's law and living in honesty.

Peel away the layers and probe little deeper
To find a man of humble demeanor,
Chaste and just in belief and manner,
Exalted as Jesus' foster father.

A man of faith in the promptings of the Spirit
Lived a life of sacrifice and forbearance,
In deep recollection and severe penance
That his actions may obtain him merit.

To guard the humanity of God's own son
Was the duty of Joseph the innocent
Who believed in dreams but ever vigilant
To protect his Mary and the Divine One.

98. Mary of Bethany

Bareness wrapped her human form,
Men dressed her up with craving lust,
Yet accused her of defying the norm,
Wanted to stone her in fake disgust.

Jesus condemned her accusers,
But absolved Mary of her offence,
In utter shame fled her pursuers,
Alone she bowed in His presence.

Drenched in torrents of gratitude,
Washed spotless of her life's stain,
And in return with love renewed
This wounded bird accepted her pain.

Her loving tears did cleanse His feet
Dried them with her flowing hair,
Kissed them at the Pharisee's treat
As she sensed their reproving stare.

Out of her means and as penance
Supported her Master and His ministry
Imbibed His words, lived in His presence
Sat at His feet in profound humility.

Her heart ached when He was crucified
Wept bitterly in desolation,
Stood by Him and felt unified,
Now a woman of seraphic perfection.

At Calvary's brow she stood by Him,
Propelled by faith and conviction,
At the tomb sang her ultimate hymn
And received her Master's benediction.

Spurred by concern to the tomb at dawn
She hurried worried to anoint His body,
Devastated to find that it had gone,
A distraught moment for Mary of Bethany.

First to meet Jesus after His resurrection,
This eternal monument erected by mercy
As the apostle of apostles received promotion,
Lived in solitude a life most worthy.

99. The Disciples of Emmaus

The two from Emmaus, trudging back
To their village along winding track,
Head hung low, dejected and forlorn,
Eyes moist, their Master they mourn.

The two obscure and humble men
Who had witnessed the Lord's Passion,
Agony, torture and death on the cross,
Were now aware of their tragic loss.

Rapt they heard his new missive
He didn't hesitate to heal or forgive,
Spoke in parables, love was His theme,
He worked miracles and had a team.

A friend to the poor and the downtrodden
Damned the Pharisees and their brethren,
With authority He taught and explained,
The new doctrine of love he proclaimed.

Submerged in guilt and shame they turned
Back to Emmaus, much concerned,
To pick up their life they'd left behind,
And be accused, taunted, and maligned.

They must suffer the consequences
For they discarded their preferences,
And resolved to pursue their decision
To follow in the steps of the Galilean.

As they walked on deep in thought
A stranger stepped in from a side street,
Merged in with them for company.
"What's it you speak, why such a hurry?"

He got their answers and they were to listen
To the reason, the manner, and the decision
For His gruesome torture and death
That echoed long ago from the prophets' breath.

The long journey came to an end,
They were home but He took the bend,
"Stay with us and share our meal,"
He broke bread and opened the seal.

They saw the Master, felt consoled
And took wings to inform their fold
In the dead of that unexpected night,
With joy abounding in their heart.

"We've seen the Lord" their voice was shrill,
There was exuberance, there was thrill,
Jesus is risen, their Master's alive.
"The Lord is back and we will survive".

100. The Prodigal Son

This soul-stirring story palpably reveals,
When a son asks for his estate's portion,
What this indulgent father's love entails
To deal with the defiant, ungrateful son!

The father represents the Almighty One
Gracious, merciful, loving and kind,
A selfish, reprobate is the younger son,
While the elder has a Pharisee's mind.

The younger son embodies every offender,
Demands his share of the inheritance
Implying wish for the death for his father
Yet the request the father leniently grants.

He left for a far country, yet not in miles,
Only from heaven's gaze he wished to swerve
When a father's image a son defiles
To be called a son, he shouldn't deserve.

Living with harlots his living devoured
Wasted all lavishly without restraint,
Till famine and starvation overpowered
And had to labor hard under constraint.

He sold himself into physical slavery,
Did the very work he'd refused his father,
Fed pigs, a disgraceful job, all agree,
He learned the hard way and had to suffer.

He came to himself, his outlook recast,
Contrition brought him close to salvation.
In the state of a sinner reminiscing his past,
Saw his father's goodness with elation.

He gathers his rags and shabby shoes,
Plods back wearily to his father's home,
A different person with saner views
He firmly decides never again to roam.

Day after day with insatiable longing
The father up from the terrace surveyed
The distant path the son would come calling,
And his wrinkled brow the anguish conveyed.

Across the horizon a head appeared
He knows the gait, it's surely his son,
The sight of his face, all fears allayed,
With outstretched arms he began to run.

The famished son could only trudge
On leaden feet without pride or dignity,
But his aged father forgot his age
Ran and hugged and kissed him lovingly.

The repentant sinner's bond is restored
With this father, most amazing,
It reflect the essence of a forgiving God
To every fallen man who seeks his blessing.

101. Sons of Thunder

James and John, the Sons of Thunder,
Nicknames given to them by Jesus,
Fishermen in Galilee, Peter's partner,
Rough-hewn guys, who were like us.

Bold and aggressive of reactive temper,
Hopelessly human, remarkably normal,
Despite his strong and fiery nature
John became love's staunch apostle.

Ambition reared its ugly warhead
Asked for a seat on his either side,
Didn't get the approval they'd expected
And their colleagues were quick to chide.

Jews and Samaritans were on the war path
Rejected Jesus' call to radiate love,
James and John wanted to rain their wrath
By calling on them fire from above.

Their approach bold, aggressive and formal
Melted and transformed as time passed,
Became eminent ministers of the gospel,
Spread the Lord's message unabashed.

Both wrote and preached undeterred
James died a martyr, by the swing of a sword,
As the apostle of love, John was declared,
And a long and fruitful life was his reward.

102. The Holy Spirit

You are the consuming fire
That can't be taught or defined,
Set things ablaze entire
And penetrate the core of our mind.

This fire burns out the dross,
Refines to make us pure gold,
Refills us with your presence,
Illuminates our abode.

You are the water's well spring
The source of our life's essence,
Out of your innermost being
Grace will flow in abundance.

At dawn you're Israel's dew,
Like the lily he'll blossom,
To refresh nature you pursue
And revive and refill his bosom.

Your oil anoints your people,
Consecrates them your own,
Seal them for now and eternal
To keep them by your throne.

Peace, hope and joy are pleasures
Enjoyed when your Spirit arrives,
Your seven gifts are our treasures
That will direct our lives.

103. The Pharisee and The Publican

He looked at the two standing apart
One stood upright and looked on straight,
He embodied a Pharisee's behavior
Acclaiming blatantly his deeds in favor.

'I'm not like any other men you'll find,
I fast twice and pay tithes in kind,
I'm not a robber, nor an evil doer,
Nor like the man there, a tax collector'.

The tax collector stood at a distance
Beating his breast, bowing in silence,
Afraid to look up in guilt and shame
Genuine was his confession of blame.

The Lord proclaimed what the man ignored:
The self-exalted shall be put on record
As the lowest in status without dignity,
The tax collector pleased the Almighty.

104. The Man at the Pool

By the Bethsaida pool I lay wasted
Awaiting the angel to stir its water,
When the angel appeared I was elated
But my weight caused my limbs to falter.

It takes me long to drag my body
For my place isn't close to the edge,
For who are alive, alert and ready
I'm too slow and lazy, they allege.

Even if I am at the edge of the pool
I struggle and wriggle to plunge myself in,
Yet defeated, dejected I look a fool
And shed copious tears within.

'Rise', said the stranger with compassion
'Take you matt and leave this place'.
Tears of gratitude was my reaction
For he rescued me from utter disgrace.

105. The Shepherds

An array of angels dressed in white
Silhouetted the edge of the darkened sky,
When they spread their wings at night
A radiant glory illuminated thereby.

In the silence of this starlit night,
Sheltered from a chilling gale,
The shepherds kept guard to scan the sight
For robbers or wolves could assail.

An angel announced with trumpet blare,
"Fear not for your Messiah has arrived
Go to the manger, you'll find Him there,
Your long awaited Savior and guide.

A choir of myriad voices in unison
Chanted Hosannas to God's own son.
It resonated in ripples with ardent passion
Giving the shepherds a feeling of elation.

With waves of glorious song of praise
The brilliant splendor began to fade.
The shepherds had their ardor ablaze
To them was the disclosure first ever made!

Despite their humble and lowly rank
They represented the human race,
On bended knee to worship and thank
And receive abundant blessings and grace.

Reaching the cave a cry they heard,
Peeped in and saw the sleeping infant,
Knelt before the Lamb and their Shepherd,
Seeing their affinity, it was evident.

For God's ministers, a cathartic experience,
For willing listeners, a divine voice,
For the faithful and dedicated guardians
To guide and lead the flock, their choice.

106. Elizabeth

Daughter of Aaron despite her mission,
Had to undergo a time of privation,
In God she placed her unflinching trust
Her barren womb would one day yield fruit.

She found no oases of expected comfort,
And was devoid of the basics in her desert;
The mother in her painfully groaned
To hold an infant she had not owned!

She longed to love and cuddle a child
For her barren womb she was reviled,
Desolate and broken, wept her heart out,
Yet in God's providence she refused to doubt.

She didn't despair, her hope was firm,
With faith in her God she worshipped Him;
People stared at her and read her womb
A curse was written that caused this doom.

The disgrace she bore was promptly cleared
When the angel had the good news declared;
Her womb was alive with the breath of a son
And the mute father's dumbness was undone.

107. Simon of Cyrene

Simon of Cyrene was an outsider
Who'd come to observe the Passover,
But was compelled to carry the cross
And Jesus's heavy burden to endorse.

Reluctant though at first he stepped forward
Took up the weighty beam of wood,
Felt drawn into Jesus' profound pain
Received the most significant gain.

Step by step he shared the burden
An active partaker, not a bystander,
Felt the weight and purpose of his call
Grasped in some way, however small.

The immense love and sacrifice that drove
Simon to compassion wasn't in vogue,
Now it's a symbol of the way we are called
To share the burdens of the forlorn and ignored.

Simon became a Jesus follower
His Christian sons, Rufus and Alexander
Simon is defined as 'one who hears'
So his presence here aptly appears.

He heard Jesus groan and cry,
Perceived Mary for her son sigh,
The crowd jeering and making fun,
What Jesus spoke when his life was done.

People of Cyrene were also among
Strangers who heard in their own tongue
The message Pieter spoke on Pentecost,
Revealed to him by the Holy Ghost.

108. The Magi

Melchior, Gasper and Balthasar
Three wise pilgrims from afar,
On camels across the desert they came
Asking Herod the new king's name.

Rattled by the news of a new born king
Herod consulted the prophet's writing
'In Bethlehem of Judah among the Jews'
He told the wise men to return with news.

The star reappeared as a proper guide
Brought them before the new born child
Bowed in worship before their Lord
Spread three gifts they could best afford.

They had gifts of exceptional worth
Fit for the King of heaven and Earth:
Gold and myrrh and frankincense,
A unique bouquet of royal essence.

Warned in a dream they changed their route
The way was long but they didn't dispute
Avoided Herod and safely returned
Feeling converted and blessings earned.

109. Cain and Abel

There's a Cain and an Abel in all,
Discern and select the better one,
Cain is physically mighty and tall,
But ugly and repellent like a demon.

Ruthless, unforgiving, brutal in action,
He worships envy as his mentor,
Often behaves in vindictive fashion,
Revenge round him coils like a viper.

Unable to express the finer sentiments
Of love, concern, or compassion,
He prefers falsehood and resentments,
Swollen pride and hostile reaction.

Abel represents grace and excellence,
Finer sentiments of mind and of heart,
He professes loyalty and reverence,
And profound values with ease impart.

The destruction of the Cain within us
The potent emergence of the Abel,
Are all on what we need to focus
To our heavenward journey enable.

110. Bartimaeus the Blind Man

Bartimaeus relied on his ears for aid
Blind since birth in streets he lived,
Hearing footsteps and voices one day
Perceived Jesus was coming his way.

So he called out, 'Jesus, Son of David'.
A gruff voice in the crowd rebuked
For he was ugly, annoying and blind,
Deformed, uncouth, unlike their kind.

Jesus meets Bartimaeus outside the city,
Where lived the scum, the misfits, the guilty,
Places we wouldn't like them be seen,
Heals his eyes by removing the screen.

We are called to look outside the crowd
To love the lonely, oppressed, awkward,
To bestow dignity, love and respect,
And the disabled, accept and protect.

The crowd welcomes the pretty, the popular,
The well-dressed with an athletic figure,
But someone like Jesus they'll crucify
And in no way on them we can rely.

Should we go with or against the flow
In abortion, euthanasia and alike foe,
Or to love someone outside our circle,
Offer help to get over the hurdle?

Bartimaeus did not miss out the point
For his request was perfectly relevant,
Knowledge of Jesus is our advantage
In every circumstance it helps us manage.

111. Paul the Apostle

Gigantic in stature, vigorous in force,
A fearless Jew in relentless pursuit
Of people of the Way he sought to endorse
For oppression or death without dispute.

Born in Tarsus, Saul was a Roman
Trained by Gamaliel, was anti-Christian,
On way to Damascus he encountered Jesus
Heard the divine call to change life's purpose.

A missionary intrepid in every sense,
An itinerant preacher without pretense,
A prolific writer with knowledge and skill,
Is Paul, who decided to follow God's will.

Apostle of the Gentiles, born as a Jew,
Who opened the doors of salvation anew
To everyone who wished to follow the Way,
Guiding them right, so they didn't go astray.

112. The Stone in the Sling

You're a stone in the sling of the Lord
Even mightier than a fencer's sword,
You may be nothing on your own,
But his power will make you known.

David had few stones in his pocket
He took out just one for his target,
Swung the sling in a rainbow arc
And released the stone to hit the mark.

Goliath's fall brought utter dejection,
With him fell the pride of a nation,
God had employed a humble shepherd
To save a people, for ages tortured.

You aren't anymore a lifeless being
When you're wrapped in the fabric of the sling
His new energy will empower your system
You will evolve a person of wisdom.

113. The Woman at the Well

Jews and Samaritans were proclaimed enemies,
Persistent tension couldn't find remedies,
The Zebedees wanted to bring down fire
And destroy their tribe whole and entire.

Seeing a Jew at the well she feared,
Wondered how this stranger had appeared,
A man and a woman at the public well
Conversing with each other was a scandal.

He'll be defiled if they meet and talk
Being a Samaritan, of an unclean stock,
Jesus wants to knock down barriers,
Racial, religious and gender dividers.

He's after the lost sheep, the lost coin,
And the lost daughter and every human,
Ready to give fresh and living water
And fill the emptiness that makes all falter.

Were all her husbands removed by force
Or is she a tragic victim of divorce?
Whatever it was she obtained healing,
And in Jesus found purpose and meaning.

114. The First Martyr

A foreign-born Jew of Jerusalem,
Was the first to persecution succumb,
He was anointed a Christian deacon
Who often met with strong opposition.

He gave out alms and served the poor
Preached Christianity with vigor and valor
Opposed Temple cult, glorified Jesus
As the fulfillment of the Law of Moses.

A man full of God's grace and power
Performed signs and deeds of wonder,
His defense so outraged the Sanhedrin
For the Spirit's wisdom was deep within.

His opponents couldn't win a fair fight,
Used lies and secret strategies as bait
Stirred up the people against Stephen
Seized and brought him before the Sanhedrin.

He was sentenced to death by stoning,
An apt way of his actions disowning,
His face was like the face of an angel
And he appeared all peaceful and stable.

He wasn't filled with fear or terror,
For he knew his life was in God's favor
His face reflected the very same story
That Moses had as he beheld God's glory.

115. The Rich Fool

I'm a wealthy man, wise and responsible,
My land's yield has been unbelievable,
I haven't enough space in my small barns
To store for the future all the grains.

So I must pull down and erect new ones
Bigger and stronger to preserve in tons,
The bumper crop I got from my fields,
To enjoy when my body no longer yields.

I know my savings are worthy of praise
For I have my future well set in phase,
I tried to work hard and time well employ,
Now I can sit back, relax and enjoy.

God heard the rich man's conversation
Cut short his dreams to offer salvation,
'You are a fool for not reckoning with God,
You feel or express no sense of gratitude.

'All the fruit of your hard earned labor
Will end up in someone else's favor,
Your lives and possessions are not your own
As mere steward you shall be known.'

116. The Widow and The Judge

I don't fear God nor assist man
I deal out justice as I can,
None can bribe to change my plan
For such clients I've placed a ban.

A widow in town came for justice
Sought his help without malice,
Frequently knocked at his bar door
Against her rival who troubled her.

The old widow was persistent
Which made him very indignant,
In spite of his repeated rejection
To give up she had no intention.

Every strategy he employed had failed
So he couldn't her presence avoid,
But she was determined in her stand
And made his life very unpleasant

He reviewed his former decision
Got justice to her satisfaction ,
Peace of mind in both prevailed
As the final result was unveiled.

117. Veronica

A gentle woman, a fragrant follower,
Unknown, unheard, unseen before,
Distraught as she observed Him suffer
Couldn't ignore their cruelty any more.

A compelling urge to assist the victim
Welled up in her anxious heart,
Only a veil she can offer Him
To cleanse his face of dust and sweat.

Fear has vanished, resolve stood firm,
There's no turning back, come what may,
Stealthily she sneaks, she must perform,
Approaches him cautiously without delay.

With due respect before Him kneels,
Unfolds the veil and swabs the face,
The sweat and dirt she wipes and cleans
Before the soldiers could start the chase.

Oh what a rewarding experience,
What a treasure to hold and cherish,
For He imprinted His countenance
On her veil and heart to embellish.

Indelible and precious in reality,
In appreciation for daring to serve
The man she followed to Calvary,
Offered this reward she did deserve.

118. Zacchaeus

Zacchaeus was a shrewd tax collector
Who suddenly emerged on this occasion,
Met Jesus in an unusual fashion,
Perched up on a bushy Sycamore.

Regardless of his countless flaws
Cared not if he's in anyway ridiculed,
For up a tree in haste he scrambled
To see the man who preached new laws.

Impressed by his authentic act
Jesus ordered him get down at once,
Said he would dine with him thence,
A proposal that had a powerful impact.

A sudden stirring of divine grace
Mirrored him now in a different light,
Rescue entered his house that night
And formed him a man of noble race.

He confessed his weakness in front of all,
Vowed to repay those he had wronged,
And make amends to those he'd betrayed,
Thus emerged a new man, stately and tall.

119. Samuel's Calling

'Samuel', three times the boy was called
Yet he failed to discern God's voice,
At the fourth call being much appalled
Answered at Eli's wise advice.

Samuel ministered before the Lord
Pleased to be Eli's favored protégé
Spent his nights by the ark of God
Heard the call in sleep as he lay.

Three times Samuel came to Eli
Each time he was sent back to rest
At the next call he was told to reply
For he felt certain Samuel was blessed.

'Speak, Lord, your humble servant listens.
Eager to obey what you command
Though small and have no experience
On your strength I shall depend'.

God revealed to Samuel his resolve
To punish Eli and his two sons
Whose blasphemy he refused to absolve
Eli didn't order them to regret their sins.

Early next morning Eli asked Samuel
To reveal his vision, hiding nothing,
That he was prepared to obey God's will
Irrespective of the decision pending.

The story of Samuel reveals the lesson:
God hates the proud, exalts the humble,
He remains faithful despite our sin
And promises a future king's arrival.

120. St. Jude

Jude, a cousin of Jesus was declared
Saint for the Hopeless and the despaired,
As patron of the impossible was aired
By God to St Bridget and to St. Bernard.

Son of Clopas and Mary of Clopas,
Sister of Mary, mother of Jesus,
One of the original twelve apostles
Was killed in Persia for preaching the Gospels.

He spread the message with ardent passion,
Made profound changes in people's vision
Suffered bravely a cruel martyrdom
In the capital of the Persian kingdom.

Jude proclaimed the Gospel in Judea,
Samaria, Syria, Beirut and Libya,
Both in Greek and Aramaic he taught,
Together with the apostle Simon the Zealot.

Jude sacrificed his life in Beirut
An axe ended his life's pursuit,
His body now rests in the eternal city
In St Peter's Basilica in sanctity.

Pilgrims flock to his grave to pray
To obtain favors when in dismay,
Miracles here are not a luxury
For they occur quite frequently.

121. The Widow of Nain

Tragedy strikes the widow's house
Her only son has met with death,
She has no other children or spouse,
She is poor and owns no wealth.

As Jesus approached the city gate
A dead man was being carried out,
The large crowd with it was desolate
Consoling and guiding the woman about.

Seeing the widow He deeply grieved,
Felt compassion and touched the bier,
Comforted the mother of the bereaved,
Gave him back life and allayed her fear.

Filled with awe they glorified the Lord,
Admitted a great prophet had come
To visit his people, ungodly and flawed,
Who could easily to despair succumb.

122. Women in the Gospels

God entrusted first to women
Things concerning God's mission,
In history's important tidings
Their role had many rulings.

During his earthly ministry
Women had prestige and dignity,
Those who had been healed
Or from whom demons freed.

They loved Him and ministered,
Out of their own means supported,
Witnessed His miraculous deeds,
And fulfilled their spiritual needs.

It was a woman who anointed
Jesus' human feet and head,
A woman had urged her partner
To spare an innocent's honor.

Women were the ones who stayed
At the foot of the cross dismayed,
And at the tomb reached first
To anoint the body of Christ.

The first to witness his rising
Was entrusted with a bidding
To take the news to his brethren
These were given to women.

Jesus loved and respected
Women and men were trusted
Both were equally honored
With freedom they were rewarded.

123. The Betrayer

The rotting lips of the betrayer
Stamped a blemished scar
On the spotless face of the Master,
In his own heart, a mar.

The kiss was a sort of reward
For having been accepted,
Letting him sign the accord
And the wallet in charge selected.

The deafening silence of pain,
Shattered by the roar of deceit,
Throbbed through His troubled brain
As in surrender He knelt.

He looked at the disloyal man
Steadily and sternly in the face,
He knew from the start his plan
His conduct had revealed a trace.

The night was long in the prison,
The trial and verdict at dawn
Found him guilty of treason,
So a plan of action was drawn.

We too have often betrayed
But for such acts we repented,
Had the deceiver pleaded
The Master would have relented.

124. Abraham's Sacrifice

Abraham took his only son
Born to him in his advanced age,
Scaled Moriah as God had bidden
To offer him as a victim in homage.

Leaving his servants at the foot of the hill
He laid the wood on the young man's back,
The knife and fire he took, it was his will,
And built an altar on an even track.

"Where's the victim for the sacrifice?"
"God will provide", the father replied,
The wood on the altar could suffice
So bound his son and over it laid.

Holding the knife to strike he strove
But an angel bad him to halt the act,
Showed him a ram caught in a grove
For the boy's offering, a substitute.

God was pleased with Abraham's faith
Made him the father of nations, his right,
His sacrifice was wrapped in spiritual swathe
It foreshadowed the sacrifice of Jesus Christ

Abraham left his country and everyone
To follow God's call despite all odds,
Are we willing to leave our comfort zone
Follow the Lord and discard other gods?

Abraham's offer to sacrifice his son
On Mount Moriah wasn't accidental,
It prefigures the act of The Three in One
On Mount Golgotha as sacramental.

The lamb is sacrificed, Isaac was saved
By an act of God's infinite goodness
Jesus is sacrificed, our sins were waived
By the Almighty's mercifulness.

125. The Holy Rosary

John took Mary home what about you?
She looks at you delighted,
To bring Mary home do you pursue?
She seems quite excited.

Mary invites you to her garden of roses
Fragrant with the breath of heaven
In your presence her love she discloses
She's a faithful companion.

Being herself the Mystical Rose
Her rosary is a source of grace
A long-standing form of honor that grows
Faster than most other ways.

A spiritual weapon so effective always
To battle Satan's assault,
And receive a downpour of salvific rays
That helps us the Almighty exalt.

A precious ornament of exquisite worth
When on your neck it's worn,
Makes you her official delegate on earth
For thus you've been sworn.

5. THE LORD'S PASSION

Immediately after his last Passover meal, The Last Supper, Jesus took his eleven apostles to the garden of Gethsemane and entered into his passion. It was a time of extreme agony and the pain was so intense that he began to sweat blood. He was betrayed, arrested, judged and condemned to be scourged, crowned with thorns, and finally crucified.

126. Garden of Gethsemane

The garden most blessed, Gethsemane,
That sheltered the Lord in His agony,
A bushy olive tree spread its arms
To shield Jesus from impending harms.

On this garden's lap he lay prostrate
Motionless, forlorn and desolate,
In the quiet of that fateful evening
When evil men were covertly convening.

His face revealed the spiraling pain
His sacred hands were trying to restrain
For the soil he gripped offered no comfort.
And there was no one to lend Him support.

He saw Calvary looming afar,
And herd the steps of the betrayer
In whose kiss his intent revealed,
An act which His destiny sealed.

'Take this chalice, Father, if it's your will
I don't know if I can your mission fulfill',
Loneliness, sorrow and fear unfolded
And all such painful emotions exploded.

The sweat had become blood on his brow
And began to ooze out and gently flow,
The red ruby drops of infinite worth
Trickled down to hallow our sordid earth.

An angel cradled His head in her arms,
Brought him comfort and sang him psalms,
Smoothened the brow and wiped the sweat,
To reduce his sorrow and be at rest.

Tranquil and serene eyes to heaven he raised
Saw the cup held by his father unfazed
Gladly lifted his hands to receive
With this he would his mission achieve.

127. Judging God

How dared you to summon me to judgment,
A mere creature, audacious and insolent?
Of my innocence you were certain
Yet you pronounced me guilty of treason.

The hands that killed criminals in passion
Slapped my face with utter derision,
The abusive insults revealed your defiance
Your filthy spittle defiled my countenance.

Like a criminal ferocious and insane
You dragged me before the public in chain,
Stripped me off my dignity sublime
And wrapped me in your gown of crime.

You tortured and hung me to die on a cross
Despite my effort to forgive your flaws.
It's my turn now to judge and condemn you
Unless you repent and faith in me renew.

128. Scourging

It is an eerie room foreboding death
That opens wide its sinister portal,
Torture devices that choke your breath
Are used on every hardened criminal.

Two Roman beasts wearing leather stripes
Lusting to feast on the Sacred Lamb,
Lick their lips and flick their whips
Eager to scourge him, set the alarm.

Amidst echoes of insults and jeers
His sacred virgin body is exposed,
Bound to a pillar helpless he appears
The venom of hatred on him explodes.

His precious body wriggles in pain
At the sharp sting of every cane lash,
Balls, spikes and hooks on a chain
Rip off chunks from his tortured flesh.

He is copiously drenched in blood,
Which gushes down and soaks the floor,
This precious blood he decided to shed
The earth's ethos he wanted to restore.

This meek Lamb doesn't bleat in protest
For love has bound Him as a guarantee
A love that transcends the mundane test
A love He bestows on mankind free

129. Crown of Thorns

They threw upon Him a purple cloak
Sat Him on a stool and began to mock,
A dried briar twig bristling with thorns
Was placed on his head amid scorns.

A dry reed, the symbol of human frailty,
Hollow and brittle in its aridity,
Was the␣scepter they thrust into his hand
To complete a king's royal attire brand.

His tormentors were all boorish and savage,
Surrounded his throne in mock homage;
They bent and bowed in deceitful pose
Only to belittle, deride and oppose.

His face was deformed with slaps and blows
Cheeks and lips cut, had a bleeding nose,
His head repeatedly struck with a rod
And thorns sank deeper drawing out blood.

Insult and ignominy raised their hood,
His face was defiled by this savage brood
With mucky, repelling and squalid spittle
And led him in chains like a criminal.

Ecce homo! Behold the Man!
The man of sorrows, the man of failure,
The man whose message seemed peculiar,
Yet a prophet who could everyone enthrall.

Ecce Homo! Behold the Man!
The man who bestowed dignity and pride,
And love and grace in abundance provide,
The man who died that we might live.

130. Behold the Nails

Behold the chilling sight of the nails
Formed in the crucible of passion,
Where an amalgam of sins prevails
With hateful deeds of perversion.

Viciously sharp to pierce the wrist,
Crack the bones in the sacred feet,
Split the network of veins in their midst
And every effort to end in defeat.

Appalling to view its shape and size,
Foreboding is this ominous portent,
Nailing the victim until he dies
To the trunk of a tree in extreme torment.

In brutal manner the scene portrays
Unbearable to a sensitive heart,
Man's inhumanity to man betrays
The way he plays his deplorable part.

131. The Ultimate Insult

The ultimate insult to personal dignity
Is to endure a dehumanizing treatment,
Severe torture to death in depravity
And shame suffered by false indictment.

The scum of the earth, unfit to exist,
More an insect, less than human,
Yet the mighty Lord didn't resist,
Gave in and accepted execution.

Stripped to the skin and insulted,
Scourged, spat upon and slapped,
Dragged him in chains they exulted,
At his suffering rudely they laughed.

The chalice of pain had reached the edge
Like wine at the brim reedy to spill,
Adverse faculties took their pledge
To increase his agony and tension instill.

132. Nailed to a Cross

As He scaled the brow of the mount
They grabbed the cross and flung it down,
Pounced on Him and ripped His garment,
He was wrapped in our sins for a gown.

Aligned to the cross, He didn't resist,
They bound with cord each outstretched hand,
Struck the nails of sin through each wrist
And his feet to a platform to help him stand.

Hot spray of blood spat on their face
Burnt their hands too, but not their hearts,
With a thud they dropped it in disgrace
Ingloriously between two castoffs.

His body stretched to its breaking point,
Pain erupted through every pore
Screaming in silent violence to anoint
His final passage ere his soul could soar.

The death of Jesus burst upon the world,
His followers mourned in utter distress,
His risen glory blazed and the news swirled
In history's pages that none can suppress.

Cast into the junk heap of humanity
The followers had been kept at a distance,
These scruffy men now erupted in glory
Pledged Him their life despite resistance.

133. At His Death

At his body's site
Some women unite,
To keep vigil at night
Together prayers recite,
Recalling His plight.

By his body they knelt,
His pain they felt,
Sensed their heart melt,
Revered the cleft,
His blood's outlet.

Harsh the men's conduct,
The torture, an insult,
Judgment was unjust,
Decision did disgust,
Anger was the result.

His body they dressed
With fine linen wrapped,
In reverence embalmed,
All emotions suppressed,
Felt themselves blessed.

His body they laid
In a stranger's bed,
Due homage paid,
Ardently they prayed,
For heaven's aid.

134. Knock of the Lance

The tip of a lance knocked at his heart
Getting no response tore open in part,
To search for the life that He had lived
Hoping to extract if he had survived.

Peeping right in, they noticed the surge
Of blood and water in torrential rage,
Soaking and blinding the anxious lancer,
Confused and spellbound he knelt in prayer.

His precious life had risen to the throne
He'd been sharing with his father alone,
But we can find him whenever we need,
Our fervent prayers he'll definitely heed.

6. MESMERIZING EXPERIENCES

Life is an amalgam of emotions and experiences. They are of infinite shades, hues and fragrances. Some turn out to be extremely pleasurable while others leave a sour or bitter taste in our belly. Our ability to discern their nature and employ them to our advantage is what makes them our friends or foes.

135. To The Wilderness

I walked behind him as close I could
Aligned to the rhythmic fall of his foot,
Listening to the music of his breath
Which provided insight and depth.

Into the barren desert he went
Feeling lonely, desolate and bereft,
It seemed so huge and disproportionate
My littleness was swallowed in it.

'Where are you Master'? In anguish I cried,
I felt the wilderness howl and deride,
Thorns pierced and ripped my body
As I squeezed through walls of cacti.

Each rock concealed a mortal danger,
Every stone hit my feet in anger,
Fear clutched like a vice my throat
As dust filled my eyes in revolt.

Solitude, bleakness and sterility
Screamed the loudest to my misery,
I was an intruder to be feared,
Not to be entertained or endeared.

In hate the wind spat dust at my face,
Sullied with filth and blinded my gaze,
Huge drops of pain pounded my head,
My mind and spirit were unprepared.

The dark gorges gaping voraciously
Nearly swallowed me into their belly,
Wild and hungry midnight creatures
Gnawed and altered my body features.

As the sinking sun stained the dry sand
And dark and ominous shadows did expand,
Fear slithered about in search of safety
A cave then opened its abysmal cavity.

There was no sign of Elijah's raven,
Nor did Manna fall from heaven,
Water didn't come rushing out of a rock,
I was in sheer despair and shock.

Night rolled in silently almost unseen,
I dreamed of a new springtime scene,
A flower peeped out into the open
At the mouth of the cave, a good omen.

As the day dawned the desert was altered
A glorious Paradise appeared instead,
'Ah, there you are! I found you, Master,
My life had almost ended in disaster'.

136. The Relentless Hound

God's mercy is a shoreless ocean,
A vast expanse of rippling waves
Of love and grace, joy and pardon.
Infinite is the extent of his ways.

His mercy generates deep compassion,
The Cross clearly reflects His love,
He suffered torture and affliction,
His death was ordained from above.

You may offend Him, you may hurt,
Desert, reject, or push him aside,
His steadfast steps, his cares assert,
He pursues to have you by his side.

This hound of heaven is ever relentless,
Will track you down, even if you hide
On mountains or in vast wilderness,
For you're his possession and his pride.

What is your worth, oh fallen race
That he woos you and offers his love?
This awesome God of infinite grace
Has several gifts in his treasure trove.

137. Your Ways are Unusual

For some you move the stones on their trail
So that they do not trip over and fall,
But for me you permit the stones assail
And allow injury on me befall.

I know why you keep the stones in my way
You want me to ask your succor from harm,
When I'm in danger you'll certainly stay
And protect me by your outstretched arm.

When I search out for goodness alone
You permit evil to obstruct my track,
When I am anxious for light to come on
You create a milieu that's dim and dark.

We fail to comprehend your plans and views
For they're far from our concept and reach,
Far better it is to depend on your clues
And adjust our mindset to learn to beseech.

138. Endless Bliss

Superabundance of joy and grace
Coated with the fresh honey of his love
Will be provided at the banquet space
To the invitees as a gesture from above.

Pleasure and comfort are part of the deal,
Pleasure that's obtained from extreme pain
And comfort wrenched from life's ordeal,
So sainthood you can easily obtain.

Once in there you'll have complete bliss
No more sorrow, pain or worry,
Peace and content shall hug you and kiss,
It's going to be a delightful story.

139. An Unusual Trip

When the sun began to peep
Shadows went hiding,
My heart enjoyed a heap
Of warmth presiding.

My journey was weary and long
My limbs faltered,
So I sang a rousing song
Never before heard.

Birds in their nests peeped out
To hear my tune,
I began to the soar to the height
To the heat, immune.

I finished my fulfilling journey
I was on time,
On the wings of glory I returned
With success sublime.

140. A Fruitful Search

I searched for God wherever I went,
In shrines of saints hours I spent,
On mountain caves and ocean's depth
Trudged the desert's length and breadth.

I went on pilgrimage to sacred places
I needed Him for peace and graces
But heard only the echo of his voice,
And a feeling of mysterious embrace.

The Holy Land was my final resort
Visited Gethsemane, his favorite retreat,
Stayed at places he laughed or wept
But saw only the signposts he'd left.

Being desolate and torn apart
I entered the silence of my heart
Heard a whisper calling my name
I felt my entire being aflame.

"I've been with you all this while,
Walked with you closely every mile,
But to search inward you don't care
So you didn't find me anywhere.

'Man has no time, or nerve, or desire,
Or in patience heavenward aspire,
He goes where his fancy beckons,
Often returns with unhappy lessons'.

Now that I know He's right within
I shall treasure and keep Him therein,
The most precious wealth I'll ever own
And seek forever to please him alone.

I felt his warm and energizing breath,
His touch levelled the folds of my faith,
His mist of mercy pervaded my soul,
His blessings made me a complete whole.

141. To the Wooded Mountains

A pensive sadness pervades my being
Seeps through the marrow of my spine,
I feel its effect gently beckoning
Urging me proceed to a scene benign.

An aura of mystic silence and peace
Whose presence I am unable to resist,
Draws me closer offering release
From tainted images that still persist.

Jesus would often slip out alone
Tracing the winding mountain road
To sit with his Father by his throne
And before him his mind unload.

I want to tell him so many things:
My hopes, sorrows and anxiety,
Secrets, desires, failures and pains,
And live with the owner of eternity.

To sit by his side and sense his breath,
Inhale the scent of his whispers of care,
His mystical touch of celestial warmth
Oozing copiously with me to share.

He is Love, the answer and solution,
I profess him love like no other does,
He engulfs me in his prodigal vision
I melt into him as he wraps me thus.

What an abode to recline and rest
Leaning on him with firm confidence,
United with the love of my quest
Within that heart alone in silence.

142. The Stain of Silence

Why don't you speak up, you man of reason
When actions are misguided and truth hidden?
When evil is placed on a platter to consume,
On pedestals to revere with flowers and perfume?

Assert your character and honest principles,
Proclaim your values from high pinnacles,
Counter all morbid and sleazy lessons,
Ensure an aesthetic healthy ambience.

Bark like a bloodthirsty hound on a chase
Let your voice thunder and shatter all trace
Of erudite cowards who fall under pressure
Afraid to lift up an accusing finger.

Shatter the silence through a megaphone
Through a healthy and powerful lung blown
Destroy all qualms to confront with vengeance
To clean up the blemish of unhealthy silence.

143. A Perfect Pilgrimage

A weary pilgrim is plodding along
His heart filled with a sacred song,
Day and night with fervor ardent
Heading towards the sacred mount.

The way is long and arduous to trudge,
Yet the climb he takes without grudge,
The track is winding, steep and rough,
But he has will and energy enough.

Later, drained of vigor and spark
Rested on a rock along the track,
Looking up he saw the lonely tree
On the brow of mount Calvary.

Spurred on by this scene he was amazed
Fought all odds and forged ahead,
Zest gave him wings in this travail,
The summit he had wanted to scale.

Hugging the Tree of Life in prayer,
Rooted and motionless he stood there,
Willingly and gladly his body he ceded
Had his pilgrimage fully completed.

144. We Could Only Mourn

Feeble and fragile, thus we are born
We could do nothing but only mourn.
Our parents struggled so they could give,
They died every day so we could live.

The pain and anguish they felt each day
Was shared to show us the righteous way,
When age got up and health declined
They didn't hold grudge but were resigned.

They suffered rejection and deprivation
So their children find better option,
Did they ever tell you how they'd lived?
How in their littleness, pleasure derived?

Have you ever touched your father's palm
And felt the blisters without qualm?
How about the wrinkles on mother's face,
The beauty that transcended time and space?

They bridged the two shores of life and death
For children born to them was their wealth,
Between the two shores they could align
Their future, in tune with His plan divine.

145. Strange are Your Ways

You caress me with pain
Embrace me with sorrow,
Over my wounds in vain
Some sealant dust you throw.

You fill me with longing
But keeps my heart empty.
My ego is wavy and floating
My mind's plunged in agony.

You took away from me
The crutch on which I rely,
My inner eyes can't see
So in your absence I cry.

My vision is partially blurred,
My senses are benumbed,
My life's meaning you erased,
To frustration I've succumbed.

You erased my life's meaning
With an informal sigh,
My prayers you've been ignoring,
Is it your offer of plenty?

Yet in this distress and hurt
The proof of your love is concealed
Through vibes of discomfort
Your compassion is revealed.

146. A Soul in Turmoil

My soul is in turmoil
Devastated and forlorn,
The fruits of my toil
Receives only scorn.

I know not the reason,
My conscience is clear,
No faulty intention,
My words are sincere.

Deep down in my heart,
Strong stirrings of pain
Wrestle and tear apart
Life's fabric, insane.

My search for solace
Offers no reprieve,
Since it is flawless
In time I'll receive.

147. Asking for Mercy

Raising my hands to the heavens I cried
For his mercy and compassion,
Seeking his pardon for the soul defied
By my wayward action.

He's my only hope and my desire
No one can ever replace,
He is the mountain summit I aspire
To live in harmony and grace.

Beset with tempests that stir the soul
To action without delay,
Reeling under pressure yet in control
Succeeded without dismay.

With folded hands humbly I knelt
Whispered before his shrine,
Dazed by emotions I strongly felt
The urge for his love divine.

148. Keep Going

We are travelers who began a journey
From birth we moved serious or carefree,
Our destination is the finishing line
But its length or duration we can't define.

If our sojourn is a short term affair
Forced to continue even on a wheelchair,
Or if our lifeline is lengthy and exciting
In both cases our minds should be striding.

Our body's condition may bar our progress
But our spirit can lead us to success,
Care for the body we mustn't refuse
But to neglect the soul there's no excuse.

In the end body and soul we've to proffer
One will be welcomed before the other,
But in time both will merge in fusion,
What an entity's fitting conclusion!

149. A Fire Within

There is a raging fire within,
A massive conflagration,
It burns in all its force and fury
But it doesn't consume me.

It purges my body with eager move,
Sudden and outright to improve
A sin soaked soul's secret abode,
Whose worth had begun to erode.

Left without any bone or skin,
My soul was cleansed from sin
It oars to the celestial portal
To meet my God eternal.

150. Blessed are They Who Can Sing

When I hear a touching strain
I can't control my vibrant brain,
Blissful voices in melodious flow
Uplift my heart when I am low.

Music fills me with deep emotion
It is the source of inspiration
Links me with nature to be at ease
For endless joy it guarantees.

Regulates moods and soothes my nerves,
Harmonizes passions and reason preserves,
Improves health and lowers tension,
For a good sleep an ideal potion.

Most people have this innate talent
But sad to say in some it's absent,
Can't read music nor can they sing
But listening to music is soul-stirring.

151. Cling On

The weight of your unsaid words
Struck the pinnacle of his pride,
Bits of himself he lost
As no mission was assigned.

In a whirlwind of emotion
You walked away from danger,
So that we could live safe
In elegance and grandeur.

You shut yourself alone
Felt destroyed and lost,
There's light beaming warm
Waiting for you outside.

Open wide the trap door
Permit sunshine enter
We will go on undaunted
Let not life be a full stop.

Problems go and return
Follow one after another,
We may not manage all
But it'll eventually pass.

152. My Query to the Waves

When I'm lonely I roam the beach
Watch the waves and hear their speech,
They offer no answer to my queries,
If they ever do, their answer varies.

I can't find answer to why there's pain,
Why in relationships, sorrow and strain,
The innocent suffer, the wicked go free,
Why such injustice in heaven's decree?

Why poverty and rejection exist,
The mighty rich the struggler resist,
Why can't the short on the tall rely
When these can surely our joy multiply.

The answer is not in the water's flow
Nor in the shingled shores' echo,
Tune our spirit to heaven's wisdom
That can rectify our faulty system.

153. No Reason to Hesitate

DON'T HESITATE

I stopped at the threshold and hesitated,
I dared not knock at His gilded door.
Sheer apprehension my desire prevented.
Fear crawled over and struck at the core.

My faith was weak, my trust still weaker,
Glaring offences in their garish shade
Confronted me and made life bleaker,
My courage began to grow dim and fade.

A compelling force urged me follow
The love of my heart, with Him abide,
In the little tabernacle, under the glow
Of the flickering neon light by its side.

With longing, outstretched arms He waits,
Diffident, uncertain and unable to adjust
I hesitate but my fear He abates,
And beckons me to Him to proceed with trust.

His mercy's the last straw for me to hold,
So in deep sorrow I admit my flaws,
Beg His grace to enter His fold
And live the way He always shows.

Take heart, He won't spurn your act,
Your intentions are genuine and pure,
So gently tap at His door and wait
He'll take you into His cell for sure.

154. A Smile is Like a Flower

A smile is a bud unfolding
To emerge a full blown flower,
Beauty and grace diffusing
Enchants the speechless viewer.

As it blooms to maturity
Our lips extent and bulge
The face lights up its identity
And eyes in joy indulge.

A smile is contagious, alright
Its power has magical touch,
Evokes infinite delight,
It costs nothing, does much.

A smile infuses energy
And concern for people around,
Gives everyone primacy,
Its benefits are indeed profound.

We were born to smile,
Began it first in the womb,
Smiling is truly universal,
In sleep too our smiles bloom.

A genuine smile has grace,
It's friendly and trustworthy,
Shares affection and peace,
Offers a sense of positivity.

Smile is a natural phenomenon,
Conceals emotions of strain,
Is perennial without interruption,
So smile through fear and pain.

Smile between your sighs
When you're depressed and forlorn,
Penetrate your teary eyes,
And alter the sound of your mourn.

If only you can smile
When naught is deemed right,
Life is still worthwhile
Because you put up a fight.

Just like a withering bloom
Falls to the earth and finishes,
So will your life's doom
When your smile vanishes.

155. Discerning our Need

When stars bloom
Bright and glowing,
Against blue gloom
Softly patrolling,
The earth slumbers
Caressed by numbers,
Soft and soothing
By peace embalming.

Creation rests
In placid state,
Nothing arrests
Nor any dictate,
Cool and calm
No place for qualm,
Life goes along
Healthy and strong.

There's no worry,
Tension or concern,
Life is merry
Easy to discern,
Joy and content,
The only intent,
Life requires
And ever desires.

If this was the scene,
Though unlikely,
Life's existence
Would've been lively,
Peace and joy
Would then employ
Making existence
Worth its substance.

156. Life Slips Out

Like the water when held in the palm
Leaks between fingers tightly pressed,
Without asking or informing the owner,
So life slips out of hand.

Taking with it every possession of wealth,
And much of mental and physical health,
Life glides silently into eternity,
Where pursuit appears futile.

Leaving no trail to prevent pursuit
Vanishes like shadow before a light,
Baffling the eyes that find unsettled
Life is realized incognito.

157. The Statue of Compassion

The Pieta is a great treasure of art,
This awesome statue of the Blessed Virgin
Cradling her son's body lifeless and broken,
Cushioned in her lap and against her heart.

This statue evokes poignant emotions,
Mary appears very young and beautiful,
Calm and composed, fresh and graceful,
Through her son's eyes she sees visions.

Her face portrays no evidence of pain,
Nor wrinkles of agony, no signs of misery,
For his death was an absolute victory,
And for man, hope and mercy obtain.

Mary's eyes aren't wet but are sad
Her tears are exhausted, weeping for long,
She didn't want the torture to prolong
To return to normalcy she would be glad.

When our enemies distort our preference,
When despair or failures violently assaults,
Mary will help us to baptize our faults
And sublimate our Pieta experience.

158. The Little Shrine

There is a shrine at the end of the road
Well maintained, though small and old,
Passersby pause to pray at the cross
And drop a coin in the donation box.

Most people believe it's good to pay,
As token, however small it may,
For the safety they need every day
As they drive along the risky Highway.

A favorite stop for the village women
To salute the cross enshrined within,
Though they have no specific need
Yet pay homage as taught in the creed.

Elders during walk pause to rest
And children relax having played with zest,
This is a haven for comfort and ease,
At the foot of this cross all find peace.

159. Be An Amplifier

Don't just be a speaker
Be an amplifier,
Proclaim loud like a preacher
Your silent prayer.

Tell the world what you've learned
On mother's knee,
The taste of success you earned
By slow degree.

Announce the sorrow you had felt
In Gethsemane,
Your life was totally bereft
As on Calvary.

Declare the comfort you obtained
As life's dividend,
The glory and fame you gained
With love in the end.

160. Impossible to Describe Heaven

He knocked softly at the morning sky
Got no response so still stood by,
Curiosity nudged him to go and explore
So through the cloud a hole he bore.

His heart began to beat much brisker
Mesmerized he hung on a slim whisper,
What struck him was so mysterious
He lost his balance and felt delirious.

Undaunted he scrambled up once again
A trapdoor opened to let him in,
Out of sight he vanished for quite long
Even though he didn't there belong.

Then he emerged as the door opened
Beaming with excitement tried to descend,
Plunged himself down in a deadly dive
Eager to reveal what he'd seen above.

Wide was the mouth everyone gazed at
No sound was heard despite his effort,
'Each one needs to go in person
For none can rightly describe heaven'.

161. Destiny

Destiny connotes a negative view
The public in general hold in purview,
Considered often a monstrous tyrant
Waylaying the gullible unaware,
Leading them to a scene apparent
Enticing them to consent and share.

Destiny and fate both imply
A future set by an external ally,
Negative in attitude and formally rude
Destiny plays against all accepted rules,
Victory is the only result approved
The rest is discarded as worthless tools.

Destiny implies something foreordained
Often suggests a noble end.
Destiny is determined by the choice you make
So make the choice right, it's never too late,
Remove forces if your future is at stake
And for coexistence good ambiance create.

162. Pushing Boundaries

Pushing boundaries,
Believing the impossible,
Faith to uphold
The long lost world,
These are trademarks
Of our generation.

They work together
To make it happen,
There's no delay
Nor any tension,
Things are smooth
There's no obstruction.

Life moves steady on
As is earmarked,
No barrier, no hurdle
To oppose the progress,
In awe and wonder
Life goes uninterrupted.

163. God's Mode of Expression

Poetry is the language of emotions,
It is sublime in form and essence,
It resides in a celestial ambience
Blithesome as is the smile of innocence.

God speaks to us through poetic ardor
Audible only to the sensitive receptor
Strumming the heart strings in silence tinted
To stir up emotions lofty and exalted.

We too address the Almighty in hymns
Which are candidly expressed in poems,
Befitting are the songs we render
In poetic cadence of love and surrender.

Of all the modes of expressing desires
None can do better as a poem inspires,
For it contains the sum and substance
Densely compact in all its essence.

Creation is God's poetic rendering
In the rhyme and rhythm of every being,
In this dulcet flow he wants us reminisce
And enter his abode of poetic bliss.

164. The Touch of Sunshine

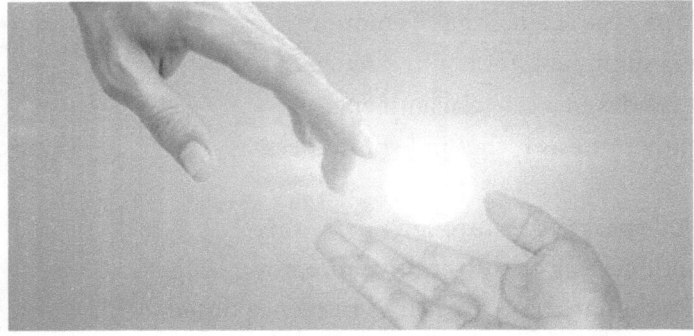

Touched by the fingers of love and care
Offered in abundance by sunshine rare,
Scattering blessings we do not deserve
Yet for the earth's sake it's ready to serve.

Winter cools down our pent up feelings
Summer brings forth the fruits of our dealings
Spring portrays nature in colorful delight
And autumn holds out a pleasant invite.

Seasons provides us with diversity,
Landscapes are conspicuous in their beauty,
Dusk and dawn are our helpful contacts
Leading us to discover unknown facts.

If we can admire the wonders of the sky
We can marvel at the feet sore and dusty,
If we can consume the cup that is bitter
We needn't wait for the one that is sweeter.

We may reject the thorns on the rose
But its color and fragrance we don't oppose,
We complain about the pollution in the air
But stop breathing it, we sure don't dare.

Our likes and dislikes are causes of tension
Which can be prevented with good intention,
An open approach to creation's largesse
Will help us attain our goal with finesse.

165. Suffering and Salvation

Is my suffering my creation
Or by way of God's decision
So to effect a true contrition
And save me from damnation?

Suffering on the altar of oblation
Is the gift offered for our salvation,
And for our lifestyle of sin and fun
Drugs and drinks posed as libation.

A sinner becomes his own enemy,
He harms himself besides many,
Those who sow evil will reap evil,
Their patron is always the devil.

166. My Precious Bird

Emerald, my precious little bird,
Though your eyes seem faintly blurred
Step out from that delicate shell,
And enjoy the new sights unravel.

I'll lift you up to balance high
Let your wing tips touch the sky,
When I look into your blue eye
No fear should it underlie.

I will provide you with wings to fly
And flying strategies simplify,
You will then flap your pinions right
And take off for your long awaited flight.

I will keep you safe in space,
You'll be secure under my gaze,
If you fly to an unknown land
My spirit will guide you by the hand.

I'll wipe away your painful tears,
Teach you through smile repel fears,
You will finally realize
These are ways your life to prize.

So fly with me, my pretty one,
Let us have our past outdone,
It was planned by the earth and sky
To urge us beyond the horizon fly.

7. EMBALMED WITH SCRIPTURAL FRAGRANCE

When we sort things out we often find certain items do not come within the purview of our decided list. We then dump them into a general items list. So we have such a list in which an assortment of topics are considered. They are equally important as the items in the regular list and their contribution is wide ranging and beneficial. They too are imbued with the flavor of Biblical themes.

167. Craving for Peace

Peace is divine and extremely precious
For a world of people turned rebellious,
The Royal Prince of peace will enable
To restore what we humans are unable.

Peace is always there free for the asking,
All around us we sense it hovering,
What we need is the right disposition,
A neutral mind receptive to intuition.

We will easily discern its object
And experience its magnificent effect,
In an ambience of solemn silence
Relying on His proficient guidance.

Peace is the rustle of shriveled leaves,
The tone we sense when fauna heaves,
The welcome shower of summer's heat,
And the slow descending snowflake sleet.

Peace is the aroma of morning flowers,
The meandering flow of perennial rivers,
The tranquil whisper we hear in the breeze,
And the buzzing hum of swarms of bees.

Peace is the vibrant colors of rainbows,
It is the twang of speeding arrows,
Peace is the sparkling eyes of the pure,
It's also the sober face of the demure.

Peace is the twinkle of clusters of stars,
The rhythmic throb of our healing scars,
Peace is the harmony of serene waves,
And the warm caress of the early sunrays.

The only requisite is to have the awareness
Of the silent promptings of peace within us,
Then the world would not only be nice
But more obviously a perfect Paradise.

168. Prefer to be Hidden

Unseen, unfelt, unheard
I wish to remain reserved,
It might appear absurd
But that's my final word.

I'm unsure of a place
That will conceal my face,
No place on the earth's surface
Nor in the sky can I trace.

No cave is deep to hide,
No chasm fit to reside,
Clouds don't screen provide
So I'm unable to decide.

Perhaps I could try
A loyal heart to lie,
On an honest mind rely,
If I fail in these, I'll sigh.

A smile would suit my aim,
In a tear make my claim,
In a heart ignite a flame,
Unseen, yet I'll be the same.

The best and safest space
Is to live in everyone's grace
In love's intimate embrace
Negativity having no trace.

169. Sin is the Skin

Sin is the skin that wraps your soul
When your heart goes wild,
You can peel or flay or condole
Or let the soul stay defiled.

Sin's like the filthy narrow road
Where you pick up dirt
It sticks to your body to corrode
And your vision to pervert.

Sin is a momentary afterthought
Escaped from your mind,
This singular provocative action left
Your soul's destiny behind.

Sin is Satan's sickle and rake
To cut and gather souls,
Feeds hell fire to keep awake
Awaiting new arrivals.

170. Sealing Scars

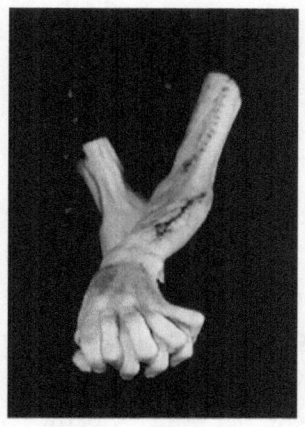

Hurts and wounds are ornaments
Laid on us by diverse agents,
The shallow ones will vanish swiftly,
The deeper remain indefinitely.

External wounds appear to heal
Faster than hurts within the soul,
The effect of both will surely result
Making a person more perfect.

Agents who often inflict these hurts
Could also be those who put efforts
Determined to destroy negative vibes
And create an ambience for serene lives.

Some can hurt with words and looks
More hurting than physical pricks,
Others heal these with only a word
Often more lasting for a long period.

Some create an autumn with a smile
Others, a winter in no way worthwhile,
Some kill people with bullet or sword
Others save those lost with just a word.

I questioned the category I belonged
Those who hurt or those who healed,
Often I found my presence in both
So now I choose the right one by oath.

171. His Concept of God

His concept of God is unique
Doesn't call God by name,
His conduct reveals the technique
He employs his faith proclaim.

Compassion for everyone,
Aid to the needy in time,
Love regardless of religion,
Are God's attributes prime.

He salutes the sun everyday
For its energy is life,
It's God's gracious ray
Even in times of strife.

For him God abides
In all he sees around,
So in God he resides
Their union is profound.

172. Some Love the Desert

It had been often the way,
Not among men of today,
To keep distraction away
Choose a desert to stay.

Sages and hermits spent
Many years in a tent,
Or in caves with intent
For their sins to repent.

They were with God in union
Their essence in fusion,
Without external intrusion
Obtain the sought solution.

Now we dread the desert,
Its effects we can't tolerate
With our improved mindset,
To value it we make no effort.

173. A World of Simplicity

Step into a world of genuine simplicity
Unpretentious laughter and candidness,
A nature unassuming mirroring modesty
Reflecting the unusual art of forgiveness.

Free from material and emotional desires,
Appreciate small things despite being rich,
Value alliance over fame of survivors,
Defend and support things that enrich.

Being ordinary yet proud of the rating,
Traditional in values most unaffected,
Old and worn out yet surrender debating,
Despite the hardship on them afflicted.

Candid and direct, devoid of hypocrisy,
Ordinary enterprise held in elation,
Informal, casual and open to query,
Plain and discreet without affectation.

Open to criticism, being informal,
Sincere and precise in all their dealings
Keeping personal attitude neutral
Without pretensions in their feelings.

Rehearsed and calculated flattery had no place
Greed lurking beneath polished exteriors
And deceptive smiles and fake embrace
Were filtered before they crossed all barriers.

Gone are those days of love undiluted,
Ambiguity wasn't held in fashion,
Deceit never any ambience polluted,
People interacted freely in the open.

Life was fresh and pure as the morning
And mind vibrant as a bubbling spring,
Serenity flowed every scene adorning
Making life lively, cheerful and stirring.

174. An Act of Compassion

Beneath a moss fringed primitive rock
Crawled an earthworm out in shock
When the earth quaked in violent mode
Shifting the position of the heavy load.

She watched the creature wriggling to hide,
Seeking anxiously for shelter it tried,
But soon flowed a deluge that shattered
Leaving the earthworm much devastated.

The girl's compassion offered succor
Steered the worm to a safer bower,
Watching it crawl and curl into slumber
Was a tender scene that greatly thrilled her.

175. Joy and Sorrow

Joy and sorrow are like the sea waves
They keep coming and going,
Their velocity often behaves
To hurt more than soothing.

Rogue waves make us wild with joy,
Crashing waves, much pain,
Surging or easing waves employ
Means to moderate our strain.

Waves make us fools as life does often
They come onward eagerly,
We run to hug them, our best option,
They withdraw from us nastily.

There's joy and pain in every wave,
It's a matter of choice;
What to reject and what to save
Will depend on one's poise.

176. Youngsters of Today

Youngsters of today are very resolute
In matters they're well versed and astute,
Despite the hurdles they daily confront
In motives and visions they're upfront.

Their ideas are rooted in reality
And are ever growing in vitality,
With depth of values in possession
They face the truth without hesitation.

They coordinate with conviction and dare,
Limitations and drawbacks they're aware,
Never retrace the step at first they took
It's always forward in their outlook.

They are convinced of power of their mettle
They can subdue foes, force them resettle
You're dazed at the way they assert
And fight for their rights ever in concert.

Young yet mature at an early age
Possess wisdom of a seasoned sage
Never succumb to enticing proposals
For they can detect even hidden signals.

Keeping decorum with dignity and pride
They can adapt and changes provide
Giants in mental and spiritual stature
They too enjoy our mundane rapture.

177. The Angelus

I rose with the sound of the church bell
That was like the call of an angel,
Urging all to hail the virgin,
The immaculate, born without sin.

A salutation most magnificent
Honoring Mary, the innocent,
Prayed thrice with fervor
Showing her love and honor.

It's a practice from ancient days
The faithful's prayer of praise,
Seeking our mother's favor
To lead us to Jesus, our Savior.

178. Offer Him a Shoulder

Infinite are the ways to employ
To help a neighbor at ruthless times,
When rumors nail him for grievous crimes
With all attempts his future destroy.

With words of cheer to take courage
And positive outlook to confront distress,
He can challenge and achieve success
If the prime factor he's able to diverge.

Offer him a shoulder so he can lean,
Swab the stains of an unhealed scar,
Embalm a fresh and throbbing mar,
And with a comforting smile intervene.

A soft caress of his tension knit brow,
A gentle touch that can even wrinkles,
Comment on cheeks with winsome dimples,
To a desperate and fallen, support avow.

Infinite are the options at hand
To name them all we need an eternity,
One at a time address each calamity
For it isn't possible to meet each demand.

179. The Mystery of Death

Death is an inevitable mystery
Like a thief he sneaks in slyly,
If you are prepared verily
You can welcome him gladly.

Avoid fear and trepidation
They serve negative emotion,
A heart in prayerful devotion
Can alter your confused notion.

Death is heaven's delegate
To lead you to the pearly gate,
Our status in honor elevate
And live in a glorious state.

You enter into life in death
By taking eternity's breath,
The door to your soul's new birth
Presents a precious wealth.

180. The Wet Pebble

From a river bed I picked a pebble
In form and shape it was spherical,
Had a surface lustrous and smooth,
This marvel did my spirit soothe.

It had stayed submerged in water,
Many waves helped its features to alter,
'Was there water within'? I wondered,
I knew it unlikely, but mind floundered.

I cracked it open with some effort,
Found its interior dry as a desert,
No sign of wetness, so I was wrong,
Though it was soaked in water for long.

Startled I reflected on my people
Steeped in tradition ever since birth,
Yet their heart was dry as the pebble
Despite living on the upper berth.

181. Under His Wings

In time all pain vanished
Sunshine cleared all shadow,
Pleasure its seat replaced,
And life began to glow.

The wings once held me as treasure
Have firm feathers reborn,
Pain is transformed to pleasure
And life with health adorn.

My love had one desire
To get a little closer
But in loving he was better
Failure wasn't an exposer.

In the shadow of his wing
My shelter is assured
No harm can evil bring
In his arms I'm secured.

182. The Process of Healing

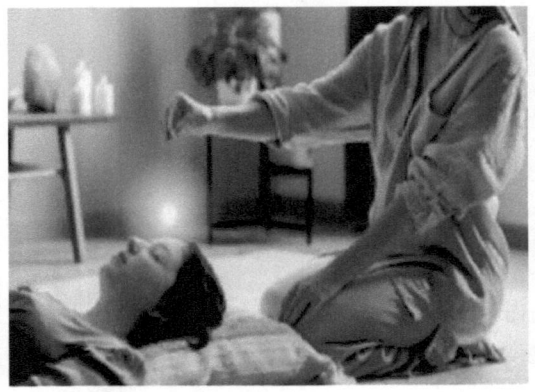

Slow in motion is the process of healing
Like morning mist enwrapping a valley,
Or like the snowflake that falls early,
The effect is always sure and enduring.

No effort is required, nor any force,
No pressure to apply during the course,
Healing is gradual, can be conditional,
Often permanent, sometimes internal.

Healing is like the prayers we raise
Which ascend to the throne of God in praise,
The response could be slow but smooth
With the assurance of our heart to soothe.

May descend gently when unexpected,
May not happen the way we requested.
In resolute faith we wait for the scope
Of a positive report in prayer and hope.

Healing may not always happen
Depends upon our worth and vision,
We need often to upgrade our condition
Bring about in us a sublime transition.

Internal healing needs urgent attention
When spirit and mind simmer in tension,
Wounded emotions destroy our future
And dehumanize our permanent nature.

Healing process can alter our vision,
Gradually change our life's only mission,
Transform a seeker to a new entity
And attain an esteemed identity.

183. True Justice

The face of Truth was grave and solemn
Within the confines of Laws' edifice,
The august receptacle that encased wisdom
Was the preferred haunt of Chief Justice

Enthroned on the seat reviewing chapters,
Scrutinizing every iota of all the cases
Related to the deeds and legal matters,
His Lordship routinely solicits or proposes.

Justice that emerges from wisdom's spirit
Sees all cases with eyes unmasked,
Deliberates upon their flaw and merit,
Passes judgment with fairness unsurpassed.

Without regard for the ethnicity,
Or any form of complacency,
Justice must not see but only weigh
And give out a verdict with clemency.

184. Which Way to Choose

The journey was strenuous, exacting and long,
I trekked the woods with a mournful song,
The road-end formed a fork before me,
Right to the mountains, left to the sea.

I surveyed them both in exceeding anguish,
The left road enticed me with offers lavish
Down a smooth track, margined with flowers
To a grand vista that attracts and empowers.

The other emerged a meandering track
Lined by thistles for a brutal attack,
A narrow gate was open to welcome
Visitors arriving there, though very seldom.

People prefer the glam and exotic,
Pleasure of every kind, often chaotic,
Unaware of its transient element;
Bless those taking the trail's rough segment.

185. The Bell Tolls

When the bell toll is repeated and slow
It often signifies someone has died,
From the sound's character we come to know
For it comes with a melancholic slide.

Everyone's death is a loss to us all,
Because we're part of every person,
Death of anyone can us appall
For it's a loss to every human.

Bells may peel at every funeral
Or at the service before burial,
Also for asking the faithful turn up,
To pray the Angelus or offer worship.

Bells had always been a sacred object
In churches to create a better effect,
People regarded bells in high esteem
For they represent some spiritual theme.

186. Glittering Tears

The glow in a teardrop is mesmerizing,
Its brilliance is unique and fascinating,
It charismatic persona thrills the viewer,
Attracts and inspires its pursuer.

Be it the sight of a tear filled eye
Or a drop dangling at the eyelid by,
Each is an object of wonder to behold
Enhancing as gentle feelings unfold.

Each drop may convey sorrow and pain
Shed for some cause we can't explain,
Or it may reflect some delight extreme
Having the tone of a pleasurable theme.

Teardrops evoke love and concern,
Treasures given free, we do not earn,
Values like compassion and tenderness,
And such others we cherish with fondness.

187. Time or Space

Space and time are intricately bound,
Space seems important for it lets us exist,
Like all life forms they are profound
And in our ventures ready to assist.

Time seems greater than any kind of space
For space is stagnant in form and shape,
It can't change its shape or replace,
Nor, on its own, attempt a reshape.

Time is always in uniform motion
Permanent and having a regular place,
Time proceeds in rhythmic progression
Resetting time will normalcy erase.

Space and time are both important,
Time helps us to structure our lives,
Create schedules and prioritize want,
In time's compass every space thrives.

188. The Language of Conscience

Whisper functions in unvoiced mode
To express secret views and news,
Share them solely through unknown code
To eliminate chances of data abuse.

Whisper is evident in nature's bower
Celestial or terrestrial in their dealings,
Spirits enjoy such divine leisure
Among themselves or with other beings.

Whispers are heard in places of worship,
In libraries where silence is observed,
Between couples during their courtship,
In graveyards where bodies are interred.

Whisper is a loyal confidant and friend,
A guide to meet when doubts resound,
With voiceless message she will defend
For she's softer than any voice around.

In the placid flow of the ocean waves,
In the thunder's murmur in low rumble,
In the silence of deep mountain caves,
Whisper takes a leisurely amble.

Heaven reveals its wishes in whispers
And its expectations in still voices,
Our response will be silent couriers
To endorse the need of making right choices.

189. At the Mouth of Hell

Walking on tip toe along the fringes
That surrounds the entrance of hell,
An intensely hot air my right impinges
And strikes my face a nauseating smell.

Peeping in I saw like torches burning
Bodies of people enveloped by flames,
From the inferno erupted cries of suffering
Unbearable beyond any human claims.

Why do people go into this hellhole
Even though they know what's in there?
Man needs help to alter his goal
To desist from sin and avoid despair.

190. No Time to Die

I have done all that I ever wanted,
What was asked too I have completed,
Now I want to die in peace and quiet,
But where's the time to die and depart?

Many needs arise and sneak in abruptly
Caution is needed to handle them promptly,
But the flow is never ending to my dismay
And it's the cause of my departure's delay.

Heaven in good measure, running over,
Is poured onto me as a worthy proffer,
Declining it could pose an affront
So I am helpless on every count.

Confidently I am awaiting my turn,
To bolt away to him ardently I yearn,
Each moment bubbles with fervent desire
Waiting for His call to go up and retire.

8. BEAUTY OF A SOUL IN GRACE

By definition of the word grace one can understand that a soul in the state of grace is extremely blessed and is immensely pleasing to God. Such a soul reflects God's own attributes.

191. Messages in Her Smile

Instant and spontaneous was her smile
A mystical outlook revealed its profile,
It arose from within and colored her face
Its soothing aroma pervaded the space.

Lavishly this precious gift she offered
To every visitor who eagerly lingered,
For they felt enriched by her acceptance
And candid approval of their presence.

Her smile was an enigma hard to construe
With varied shades and contents in queue,
Though sweet, gentle and deep in essence
An ethereal dimension wrapped in defense.

Her smile revealed her intrinsic beauty
Where innocence merged with simplicity,
And profusely served out without restraint
Devoid of guile or cynical constraint.

Her smile was genuine revealing her desire
To set the world of sadness on fire,
Radiate passion for unity and trust,
And avoid emotions of hate and distrust.

A positive bonding her smile inspired
Her words of wisdom, much admired,
Keeping her company was a pleasure
Like a worthy shrine owning a treasure.

192. She was a Jewel

There is a beauty beyond the senses
And that is what she was blessed with,
Strength and honor formed her pith
For she refrained from all pretenses.

A beautiful jewel, rare and treasured
Her soul a brilliant glow diffused,
The wine of desire in her infused
A thirst for every heart unmeasured.

The memory of her passing appearance
Left an indelible scar on my heart,
Love for her wasn't a form of art,
But a deep penetrating fervent radiance.

193. The Scar of the Tear

At the foot of the cross alone she knelt,
It was a heart wrenching agony she felt,
Pondering over the passion he endured
And the painful torture he had suffered.

From the opened wound within his heart
Sprang up a yearning to love impart,
From her woeful eyes hot tears emerged
At the eyelid's edge so they lingered.

She felt impelled to inhale his vibe
And pined anxiously his agony imbibe,
A teardrop suddenly fell on her chest,
Forming a deep scar, her welcome guest.

Heaven was sharing her pain entire
That she sealed with the balm of desire,
The lilting rhythm of her eternal thirst
Was throbbing ardently within her breast.

This scar wrapped her in a snug embrace,
Its soothing touch had the fullness of grace,
Immersed herself in this blissful scene,
A thrill through which she'd never been.

She entered the eye that had shed the tear
And found her eternal lodging in here,
Though still kneeling at the foot of the tree
Her fervent spirit was blissful and free.

194. A Melodious Symphony

She was a melody swaying with delight
On blithesome wings that took to flight,
Even beyond the horizon's crest
Where angels and fairies flocked to rest.

Her music sailed like the velvet fleece
Gaily on the breath of whispering breeze,
Leaped with abandon like stags in parks
And kept abreast with the call of larks.

Her strains had a touch of grief and pain,
Pulsated in anguish, the haunting refrain,
Her melodies weaved a web of unity
Hugging everyone in deep serenity.

Her numbers thrilled an unbiased audience,
Consoled the rejected, diffused radiance,
Every verse followed a dulcet chorus
Laying a loving testament before us.

195. Her Apprehension

She stopped at the threshold and hesitated
Dared not knock at His gilded door,
Sheer apprehension her wish prevented,
Fear crawled over and struck at the core.

She'd come crossing wastelands of misery,
Moors of vague and shallow values,
Deserts of ignorance and vales of treachery
Scaling peaks hostile and walking through refuse.

Her faith was weak, her trust still weaker,
Glaring offences in their garish shade
Confronted her and made life bleaker,
Her courage then began to dim and fade.

A compelling force then urged her to follow
The love of her heart, and with him abide,
In the little tabernacle, under the glow
Of the flickering neon light by its side.

With longing, outstretched arms he awaited,
Diffident she was and unable to adjust
Hesitated but her fear he abated,
And beckoned her to proceed with trust.

His mercy was the last straw to hold
So she repented and admitted her flaws,
Pleaded for grace to enter his fold,
Was accepted with a mighty applause.

196. A Resilient Life

A vibrant and resilient life she lived
Over the troubling sea of doubt,
Pain was the road she trod to shield
From the swelling storm spreading about.

She wasn't here by mere accident
But was led here as God had willed,
For his grace came at the right moment
To have in her heart faith instilled.

Over the edge of conscious delight
Repentance curled beneath the gale,
A timely mediation seemed to invite
From guilt of flaws in sorrow bewail.

A critical moment of trust prevailed
Over confusion, fear and descent,
The new daylight a highway unveiled
A bright future she never had dreamt.

197. Distraught and Lost

She sat and stared at the vacant chair,
A deluge of pain harrowing and intense
Distilled through the sieve of despair
Crushed her heart with pain immense.

That chair was his favorite haunt
Customized for his crippled state,
Now disturbed as his memories daunt
She feels devastated and desolate.

He was just ten, a tender age,
Died of cancer, having not lived,
With anxious care she tried to assuage
The severe agony he had endured.

Alone with his shadow unseen or felt
Believing to be in an alien ambience,
Her wilting figure she hid and kept
Until her mental sanity found credence.

A day dawned when her feelings erupted
Like a volcano for long dormant,
The molten lava flowed uninterrupted
Leaving trails from her eyes in torrent.

Life had rotated a complete circle
On despair and sorrow to reach reason,
Having returned to a life of the normal
She began weaving a tapestry of her own.

198. The Chalice of Pain

The chalice of suffering was filled to the brim
When she sang her final hymn,
It spilt over and drained out all pain
All along she'd been struggling to restrain.

Her life was like a bag of good fortune
Everyone seeking to share a portion,
Cold and unfeeling they were of heart
Ready to wrench even her body apart.

Like a grape, purple, ripe and swollen
Squeezed by evil into submission,
Filtered through the sieve of anguish
Poured into her chalice a portion lavish.

Simmering in a cauldron on a hot fire
Her resolve to resist surged even higher,
Firm and unflinching wielded a new helm
That helped her rise to a superior realm.

199. In Your Presence

When I sit before the Blessed Sacrament
I feel I'm in a world very different,
I may be happy or I may be sad
But in your presence I'm ever glad.

Whatever is in mind I can talk about
Without hesitation or any doubt,
For I'm certain you don't take offense
And the joy I receive is truly immense.

When I speak of some unbearable pain
And expose unsure I suspect the reason
I realize how easily you understand
So I am relieved to have you at hand.

When I'm heartbroken, lost and forlorn
I withdraw inward and helplessly mourn
But your presence gives me consolation
Helps me regain my normal disposition.

Your unspoken words, strong faith impart
And the stirring of love within my heart
It's beyond all gifts I may ever need
That's why I follow every step you lead.

Often on knees I confess my sins
To secure for my soul all needed gains
This is when your grace envelopes me
Cleansing my soul and from sins free.

Even when I am on my way home
Having paid the needed ransom
I feel your blessing hover above
Leading me closer with urges of love.

Spending time with you is a blessing
For I feel you Jesus I'm possessing,
In life that is the ultimate purpose,
The only means to heavenward spur us.

When I sit before you in adoration
My mind is steady and purpose driven,
Calm and composed I make decisions
And for my problems, find solutions.

Here you interfere in my affairs
And guides me select the correct ways,
I need you Jesus all day and night
That's why I come to you at the first light.

200. Get Down to Your Knees

The shortest leap to sanctity
Is just to fall onto our knees,
The same knees with tenacity
We struggled on in our infancy.

Once on our feet we'd started
Seldom we thought of them,
Though for motion discarded
Refused utterly to condemn.

Often we fall onto our knees
When pardon and help we need,
For faith and hope to increase
On bended knees we plead.

We hurtle down in courtesy
Before his awesome presence
Into His ocean of mercy
And unite with his essence.

Get set and leap onto your knees,
Bow down and receive a blessing,
Promise to follow his decrees
For he's your Lord and King.

201. He Kills the Sting of Pain

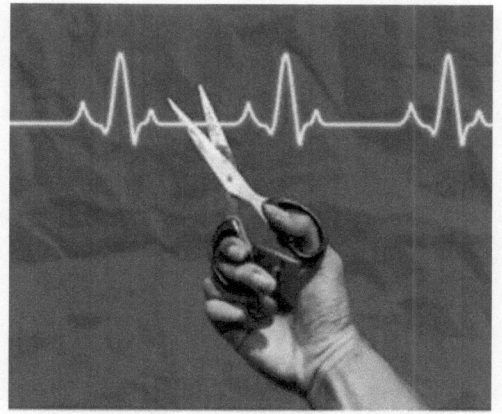

He's like a reed on the edge of a hill
Struggling to stay on upright and still,
Wind pounding him mercilessly harsh
With thunderbolts during a lightning flash.

His creaking knees are hollow and weak.
The spine is slender, the vertebrae squeak.
He twists and turns and writhes in pain,
Discreetly conceals his struggle in vain

He turns them into redemptive suffering
To enhance their merits and obtain blessing,
He kills the sting of pain in its rawness
Willingly accepts it with full awareness.

Pain can't subdue or demoralize his ego,
Doesn't ask to be healed or pain forgo.
He spends hours visualizing his agony
On his way from Gethsemane to Calvary.

202. When She Lost Her Mother

After she lost her mother at six
She withdrew into a shell,
Or went highly emotional,
Caused by varied external conflicts.

She would stare at every woman
And appeared lost,
Often bitterly wept,
Revealed a nervous disposition.

With a heavy and compassionate heart
Her tender hand I held,
Hugs and cuddles helped,
To provide the needed love and comfort.

'You see flowers all wither and fall,
Sea waves come and go,
Like a fading rainbow,
Likewise all pain and losses appall.

'But then you see fresh flowers bloom
New shoots sprout,
Colors break out,
The warm sunshine wipes out the gloom'.

In me, her teacher, she found a mother
Always sought me out,
Never left my sight,
Our fondness and intimacy helped her recover.

I can see her now growing up well
A girl of beauty and form,
Immensely loving and warm,
Forever she will within my heart dwell.

203. He Was a Mystic

He was a mystic highly regarded
Beyond any other known,
Immersed in complete union,
With celestial vision he was supported.

Flesh and blood was without power,
Only the spirit governed
When he was summoned,
To live in the realm of the Anointer.

He fed only on the celestial bread
And the blood on the altar,
From the Lamb's slaughter,
A meal that was of unusual spread.

Alone in silence and away from all
He lived like a recluse,
Day and night to use
For progress the grasp of the spiritual.

204. Pleading For Aid

When my life is engulfed in darkness
Preserve me in your incubator,
My paralyzed mind's stimulator
Should not euthanize my helplessness.

Do not stifle my waning fervor,
Utterly spent, I reach the summit,
And this bank note I do submit
Signed and sealed in your favor.

Like a lamb caught in the cleft of rocks
Desperately awaiting a rescue miracle,
I sought suggestions from an oracle
To get over all my pitfalls and flops.

Rescued from this cosmic loneliness
Shredded, mutilated beyond reckoning,
I found in suffering purpose and meaning
Despite the onslaught of ache and distress.

As the spring of life returned afresh,
From murky darkness color broke out,
Creation throbbed with a vibrant shout,
I felt freed from the entangled mesh.

205. Attitude to Pain

God speaks in a hushed tone
When he sends us pleasure,
But pain is his megaphone,
He blares it out, his treasure.

For her thus was the design
Made her suffer in silence,
She made her pain a shrine
And burnt suffering as incense.

She placed her pain and tears
As victims of love on the altar,
When assailed by fits of fears
She prayed out of the Psalter.

The greater the agony she bore
She asked for pain more intense,
To endorse the love held in store
And keep the truth in suspense.

206. Your Warm Smile

Your smile is warm and pleasing
Suffused with positive passion,
Its innocence is ever appeasing
Spreading love and compassion.

Healthy and strong is your smile
With genuine desire to give,
Perennial and without guile,
A privileged gift to receive.

In times of doubt and pain
When sorrow pricks our nerves,
And tears flow without retrain
Your smile, our cool preserves.

A smile is a crucial factor
To boost a sagging existence,
To turn it a catalytic reactor
Is to make all the difference.

9. GOD AND MAN – A UNITY

God's expectation from man is manifested in many ways. Man's dependence on God is an undeniable reality. Both God and man maintain a deep relationship. Man's need for God is expressed in his attitude and approach. The human heart yearns for God and this is revealed in the manner in which it seeks and interacts with God.

207. Render an Account

Light me like a match on a candle
Consume me with your fire of love,
Let me carry that torch to kindle
And start a conflagration alive.

Let your fire play upon my heart
Frozen in the winter of tepidity,
Melt and restore its original part
And flow on with vivacity.

Let it burn and purge its essence
And share the effects of its sacrifice,
In its aftermath for the consequence
We'll need to pay an exorbitant price.

He took the seed of hope and gave us,
We need to transform it into a forest,
Using our talents should be our focus
He'll want an account before we rest.

208. To Sit At His Feet

I want to sit at your feet and listen
To truths you often love to deliver,
Grasp the real essence of your vision,
Enjoy the tone of your soothing whisper.

Your potent words of wisdom and insights
Help me to pursue true spiritual growth,
The profound depth of your love ignites
My heart to take a solemn oath.

I want to carve out time for reflection
Savoring your intoxicating fragrance,
Imbued with every sacred emotion
Enjoy a sense of profound reverence.

The soft glow of the flickering lamp
Casting a dim light on your tabernacle,
In prayerful demeanor here I encamp
As a sacred stillness envelops the chapel.

In this gesture of devotion I enroll,
And timeless echoes of love I profess,
Seeking food for my starving soul
Pleading my being you'd infinitely bless.

209. When I'm On My Way

I know when I go, none will bother
A sudden eclipse will usher my end,
Some may recall my actions in honor
For I had only a few to befriend.

The past is a fine place for me to survey,
To recall to mind my unusual ventures,
But not a place good enough to stay
Only an interim ambience it renders.

Some of the moments we'd left behind,
The hardest and the most distressing ones,
Come round our funeral just to remind
We failed to complete the count of our runs.

We may have dreams and daring ambition,
It would be better they stay unattained,
Once they are fulfilled, they have no passion,
Their drive and energy are by then rained.

The present leads us to our journey's end,
Unruffled and unnerved, it's better we blend,
Become a unit that can comprehend
That eternity is waiting for us to spend

210. Talk to Him Without Delay

Extend today your arms before him,
Talk to him softly deep from your heart,
Tell him of things scary and grim,
And the way they rip you apart.

Ask him for help, he'll won't refuse
With open arms he waits for you,
Talk to him of your defeat and loss
And the cost of pain endured too.

Ask him why he seems so very far
From a soul that loves his grace,
And is sincerely sad for the scar
Entreating his blessings to erase.

Did you truly talk to him today?
I wonder if he heard what you said!
Is there a reply when you pray,
Or just a silent void instead?

Speak to him when your eyes are in tears
He will listen to your prayers for aid,
Remove worries and allay your fears
His reply is certain, but can be delayed.

Tell him about your friends and foes
And the way you cope with their nature,
Lay all before him for he knows
In your heart no malice you nurture.

211. *In the Throes of Pain*

I'm startled and greatly amazed
How you load me with kindness
Dote me with gifts and happiness
At your goodness I am dazed.

What's in me to deserve your grace?
I possess nothing, can't offer a thing
A poor beggar in misery and disgrace
In return your gifts I now bring.

Every good in me is your gift
I possess only evil and sin.
Your love floods me, I must admit,
Generates faith and hope within.

My back aches, so do my knees,
Spondylitis my shoulder and neck
Varicose veins are as bad as these
Even a short walk makes me a wreck.

The stent in the heart needs attention
It has been there for quite a while,
Pressure and sugar are reasons for tension
They fluctuate in manner most hostile.

Despite these ailments I feel normal
My chores are done as they must be,
Thank you Lord for favoring me well
For eight decades keeping me happy.

212. He Made Me Eternal

Deep in the mire I was alive
Gasping for breath trying to survive,
Struggling desperately to surface
Having lost all life's purpose.

Hope appeared as just a dream
I sank deeper in despair extreme,
A sudden splash, I felt a shudder,
A cross then slipped from his shoulder.

His hand was gentle and firm
He pulled me up with his arm
The mire was no more in the marsh
He had leveled it by the splash.

He left the ninety nine to seek
The lost and wandering sheep
By a transformation internal
He made me forever eternal.

213. You are Prodigal

I sit before your picture
Reading the Sacred Scripture,
Your look brings me delight
Your words are alive and bright.

The whisper of your breath
Sweeps over me with warmth,
My joy I cannot contain
For it's beyond the mundane.

The mystical touch of your fingers
Has a soothing effect that lingers,
Your mercy hugs me with fragrance
In awe I stand in your presence.

Immersed in your embrace
I obtain the needed grace
To defend the reality
Of your Divine Mercy.

Prodigal are you with gifts
To receive it everyone insists,
It's wise to you we surrender
And live with you in splendor

214. The Altar of the Cross

We sit before the Sacred Host
For veneration exposed,
The Lamb of God, the victim,
Sacrificed for his kingdom!

The cross was the altar he chose
To lay down his life for his foes,
Now he's enthroned on the altar
We sing him hymns from the Psalter.

He hears everything we whisper,
He knows the cause of our whimper,
We may prefer to be silent,
His concern for us is vibrant.

For him words are redundant
Impartial is his judgment,
Our posture defines our ego
That's enough for him to know.

215. The Holy Sacrifice

Adam and Eve sinned in their body
So their body was rejected by God,
A new body was to be prepared,
The body hung on a wooden rod.

When the angel of death arrived
He saw the lentils stained with blood,
The blood of a lamb meant to provide
Protection for a family's pride.

If the blood of an ordinary lamb
Could a people's enemy disarm,
The blood of the Lamb slain for us
Will be sure protection from all harm.

The revered blood of the lamb we consume
Washes away the sins of the world,
Its presence within us surely will bloom
Diffusing the fragrance of his Word.

The host we receive on our tongue,
Being the flesh of the tortured One
Can nourish and brace the old and the young
Against the seductive bait of Satan.

It is at Mass that eternity meets time
And we're invited to share eternity
And this time is most prime and sublime
Forming all elements of a community.

216. The True Bread

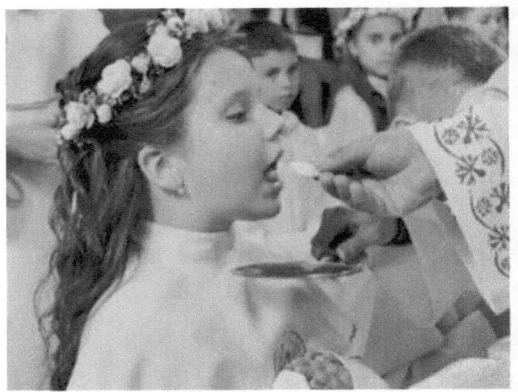

Like a dew drop that alights gently
And spreads on a tender leaf evenly
The sacred host descends and rests
Silently on my tongue and melts.

It permeates my entire essence
Transforms me anew by its presence,
Day and night it stays within me
Never leaves me to mourn in agony.

I feel our heartbeats synchronize,
His whisper seeks me to divinize,
The odor of his breath weaves around
I inhale its freshness pure and profound.

217. Waiting for the Call

Like warm waves of water
Ebbing away in soft whisper,
Like the cool mist in winter
Sieving through green pasture,
My breath is gently gliding,
For the pearly gate it's aiming.

Silver streaks sparse yet long
Privileged to my head belong,
Ruffle a mellow farewell song
In unending cadence prolong,
Wanting to keep me company
Till I embrace my destiny.

My journey is a little delayed
Extend my hour of sunset I'd prayed,
Felt it wasn't yet time to fade
Leaving my debt to God unpaid,
Having settled my account now
For the final call I bend and bow.

218. Called to a Benigne Scene

A pensive sadness pervades my being
Seeps through the marrow of my spine,
I feel its effect gently beckoning
Urging me to proceed to a scene benign.

An aura of mystic silence and peace,
Whose presence I'm unable to resist,
Draws me closer offering release
From tainted images that often persist.

Jesus would often slip out alone
Tracing the winding mountain road
To sit with his Father by his throne
And lovingly to him his mind unload.

I too want to share with him my gains,
My hopes, sorrows, fears, anxiety,
Secrets, desires, failures and pains,
And live with the owner of eternity.

To sit beside and sense his breath,
Inhale the aroma of his whispers of care,
His mystical touch of celestial warmth
Oozing copiously with me to share.

He is Love, the answer and solution,
I profess him love like no other does,
He engulfs me in his prodigal vision
I melt into him as he wraps me thus.

It's an abode to recline and rest
Beside him with firm confidence,
And with the yearning of my quest
To share with him this feeling in silence.

219. Fill Me with Your Grace

I abandoned you my Lord
Became a stranger to behold,
Went after futile pleasures,
Sin was one of the measures.

Pin prick me with your grace
Diffuse this volume of disgrace,
Empty out unchaste objects
So nothing my interior infects.

From the stable of my heart
Repulsive stenches emit
Filth my floor profanes
On walls drip down stains.

Finally I have dethroned
Everything I had owned
Now there is ample space
So, fill it with your grace.

The little that's mine I bring
To you as an offering,
That little in your hands
Increases and expands.

I'm fragmented and distorted,
My every member isolated,
Knit these pieces together
And make this unit your treasure.

Hold me intimately close,
On you let my soul repose,
Enlarge my heart for space
All unholy agents replace.

How dare have I presumed
Without being consumed
To approach the blazing inferno
Of your presence, I don't know.

Let the blazing heat of this flame
Remold my heart and reclaim,
Make it even more malleable
To bow and bend to your will.

www.ingramcontent.com/pod-product-compliance
Lightning Source LLC
LaVergne TN
LVHW091616070526
838199LV00044B/823